D.

I would like to dedicate this book to not only those that have broken my heart, but to those that have put it back together again as well. The mixture of recklessness and compassion has inspired me in ways that I am eternally grateful for.

I would also like to dedicate my words to my followers, for not only sticking by me when my poetry was amateur at best, but for loving me through every weight I put on their shoulders upon posting a new piece.

Thank you, from the bottom of my heart, to everyone that has stayed. To everyone that has reminded me that writing is healing. That writing is breathing. That my writing can change lives. I am forever blessed.

ACKNOWLEDGMENTS

Thank you, Mother, for making me wise through
your stories of past mistakes.

Thank you, Father, for teaching me strength upon
your absence.

Thank you to my family, for reminding me that
home is a heartbeat, and that I am welcome in your
arms anytime.

And thank you to my friends, for protecting my soul
when I wanted nothing more than to set it on fire.

I owe my life to everyone in it.

"you can't breathe - so you write."

"the human skin can be hard to live in"

"that's why most of us tear it open"

My name is Alexa Marie. I enjoy starting my sentences with non-capital letters and leaving out punctuation when I'm venting or writing a long, heated argument. I adore the color black. I like the look of numbers when they're spelled out rather than just written in their regular form. For example, I'm nineteen, turning twenty on the sixteenth of December. Speaking of December, my favorite holiday is Christmas. I enjoy leaving out explanations and letting others interpret something on their own. I get frustrated easily, for I always feel as if I'm in the wrong. My eating schedule is determined by who I'm with. I don't like being tied down to one thing knowing that I cannot change it. I like time, and the way that it somehow controls us. I admire the concept of inevitability and how the word 'temporary' makes me feel both worried and relieved at the same time. I don't like to speak, which is why I've always taken a liking towards writing. If something's wrong or I'm having a bad day, you practically have to pry the words out of me. I'm not good at keeping the tears in and I hate crying in front of people. I think I'm weak sometimes. My favorite number is two; I do everything in pairs. I've always loved the comfort of walking around barefoot in my house, but I've recently become accustomed to a pair of little black slippers that I never take off. I like sleeping with a minimal amount of clothes on. Loud noises scare me. I'm afraid of heights and I'm also claustrophobic. I like when people give their opinion on something without coming off as rude or arrogant. Big words used in casual conversation make me smile. I love my two dogs and my family very much. Although there always seems to be a bit of tension between those that share a part of me, we could never let it completely shatter the love we all feel. I like long showers that are hot enough to burn my skin. I dislike people that think they're always right, or people that aren't willing to compromise. I have to keep my nails painted or else I'll bite them. My mood fluctuates often, usually annoying those that are constantly around me. All I want is for people to like me, and when they don't, I feel as if there is a part of me that is more flawed than the rest. I enjoy car rides without a destination. I'm a freshman in college, majoring in journalism. I have a deep compassion for those who aren't given a second chance (for the right reason, of course.) I love sunsets and black coffee. I find an innocent beauty in the act of hand holding and an admiring stare towards those embraced in the arms of another. I don't like change. I get anxious when I have to do things on my own, things as simple as talking to an employee or calling my doctor. I don't believe that there is good in everyone. I often show signs of remorse for absolutely no reason. My voice gets really high pitched whenever I try to lie. I'm a

hypocrite in many different categories. I dislike
long nails and I hate the taste of morning breath. I
live for late night phone calls that last until the
morning and heart-to-hearts that occur along the
way. I fidget with my fingers and my necklace
whenever I'm faced with an awkward situation. If
I'm embarrassed, I'll laugh nervously and try to
redirect everyone's focus. I love the cold. One of
my fears include living an inconsistent lifetime. I
like making people smile. I dislike spicy foods and I
hate any type of fruit or vegetable. I sit cross legged
on chairs that allow me the room to. Eye contact
makes me nervous and I usually end up looking at
my feet. My goal in life is to make something of
myself, be heard, be admired. I don't think I'll ever
be fully confident with my looks or my body, but
I'm trying, and I believe that the act of trying is
enough. I'm afraid of disappointing someone that
believes in me. Music keeps me sane, and I can't go
anywhere without my headphones, nor do I ever
take them out. I'm very observant; I like to people
watch. I think that compliments on physicality's are
overrated; I'd rather be admired or praised for my
personality. I like photographs, curse words, tattoos,
and originality. I say sorry too much, I laugh way
too loud, and I tend to avoid mirrors. But that's just
me. Who are you?

they say that smoking is bad for your lungs
and that the truth will stain your teeth
but nothing is sweeter than the feel of your breath
and the way you lie to me

you are made up of lyrics and stars and laughs,
accustomed to midnight and year-old photographs.
you are lightness and darkness and everything in
between;
you are the wonders in the distance
that can't be touched,
but always seen.

This porch will someday be another's,
For one day I will grow.
I'll leave behind the swings and seats,
And every detail that I know.
I've sat here many days in Summer,
And watched the rain lightly fall.
Someday I'll watch from a different view,
But it won't feel like home at all.
Memories have been made here,
Upon this gentle, old green floor.
And everything that I see right now,
Will one day be no more.

after you left i wrote about you a lot
because it was better to have you down on paper
than to not have you at all

and later that night i burned the paper
because i remembered that you had left for a reason
and it wasn't fair to keep a reason alive
when the logic behind it wasn't

You wear a rubber band around your wrist thinking that no one notices, but I do… and I know that it wasn't meant for tying your hair up because that shit hurts when you try to take it out, and I know that it didn't just magically appear there as if for show; you wear it thinking that no one would expect you to use it as a weapon against yourself, but every time you pull it back and release it you are allowing a hurricane to take place on such a weak and fragile piece of skin, and I happen to notice the aftermath.

You go to the bathroom after every meal and it's no coincidence. I notice the way you take minimal bites and then excuse yourself, thinking that no one can hear the way you keep the faucet on just a little too long in an attempt to drown out the sound of you throwing up the remains of what you just ate. You are allowing a river of an important survival necessity to flow from your throat, not even caring about the aftertaste or the way you are ruining your fingernails. I happen to notice the distant look in your eyes and the way your fragile hands can't stop moving as if to distract yourself from knowing that what you do on a daily basis is wrong.

You can't keep your eyes open in class and you tend to lose focus during lessons and you think that no one notices, but I see you. I see the way you use your hand to keep your head up as if it's pure agony to let it go on its own. You use the same overused excuse when asked what's wrong... "I'm just tired," you say, but there's an underlying cause to the feeling of tired that you are experiencing and I am familiar with it.

You think because you sit alone and don't attempt to communicate in any way that people aren't going to give a second thought about you, but that's not true. You are allowing the dark hole that lives in your mind to grow and you don't even care. You want it to grow to the point where it swallows you whole and the only thing that remains is the small bit of hope that you didn't let anyone see for the fear of it being crushed. I see you, you are not gone unnoticed.

And it hurts me to know that too many people are experiencing the rain when they deserve to feel every color of the rainbow.

I am the darkness; I wonder why my stars aren't shining?

I hear footsteps, but I can't make out an imprint on the ground.

"I want to be wanted." I say.
"I want to be loved!" I scream.

I pretend that they care; I feel as if they do, but I don't think that they have human emotions.

I touch the cold; I worry that they are attracted to frost bitten lips.

I cry for those that have been found, for it's not always so pleasant.

I understand that the voices have to get louder; they want me to listen.

I dream that they will fall silent; I try to remove them through the veins in my wrists every night.

I hope they will leave, but I know that they won't.

I craved their presence; I asked for it, but now I'm just afraid.

I don't want to be wanted anymore.
And oh god, I can't stand being loved.

Humans will do anything to numb the pain, to forget all the bullshit in our lives even if it's only for an hour... to rid the thoughts that seem impossible to make go away.

We'll fuck a stranger we met at the bar.
Wake up to the scent of a one-night stand and sneak out before the other wakes up.
We can't feel a thing yet we can fuck for hours, calling out anything but the person's name because we didn't care enough to learn it, nor did we anticipate ever having to say it again.

We'll drink and do drugs with someone we thought was our friend only to wake up the next morning in a dark, abandoned living room.
We can't stand the thought of being alone yet we set ourselves up for it. Never noticing the distant stare in our friend's eyes or the way they shoved their apartment key into their back pocket in the midst of getting us high.

Humans will cut open their wrists with any sharp object they can find in hopes of emptying out the feeling of numbness. Of stupidity. Of regret.
It's funny, thinking that we can release the pain through our skin when really it's inside our heads.

It's screaming at us, warning us, but we're too stubborn to listen.

We'll become a slave to others, doing whatever we're told in an attempt to fill the absence that we've created.
Humans want to become something greater than the dirt that people walk on, but sometimes being stepped on is safer than growing around toxicity.

We'll try to kill ourselves without actually coming face to face with death...
but we cannot dance with the darkness and expect the music to be light.
We cannot ask for danger without preparing for the consequences first.

Humans think that they can play with the fragility of life as if it's some toy, but toys break, they always do.
And what do we do when something's broken? Fix it? Most people don't have the time nor patience to waste away precious hours trying to mend someone whose already been damaged for years.

We are all toys of the world, and it seems like the repair shop has been closed for decades.

I am the remaining shards of a mirror that lay scattered around the dusty floor, knuckles dripping red all over the reflection of the glass that emits an image I had never wished to see.

I am the subtle bruise that lacks charisma, but instead illuminates an average purple and black spot that many often poke at and scratch their heads as they wonder where it came from.

I am the soft whisper of feet as they travel mindlessly across the hardwood floor, carrying a subconscious body along with it, practically dragging the weight of someone who has not slept in days.

I am the hollow creek the bed makes when a restless heart caresses the sheets and entwines itself underneath this comforting sanctuary.

I am the dark thoughts that take refuge in a mind built for vivid imaginations that radiate color and passion.

I am the piercing scream that haunts the night air as you awake from a nightmare that doesn't go away even after you've opened your eyes.

I am the chill that finds safety between the cracks in the walls; the blown out candle whose flame was never bright enough to give a sense of serenity anyway.

I am the monster in the closet that you've made your parents check for several times, because you never quite believed them when they said that nothing was there the first time.

I am the storm raging on outside of your bedroom window.

The aura of insanity.

The figure in the dark, slowly creeping towards you while you shut your eyes tightly and dig your fingernails into the palm of your hand. Blood seeps out, but you don't even feel it.

I am the redundant breath of darkness.

I am here and I am there.

I am out of my mind.

I am staring at myself as my presence takes the form of two separate bodies.

I am my own worst fear, and I still haven't figured out if there is anything better than that.

Growing up I always thought that love was supposed to be beautiful.

I thought that lips were supposed to connect and that kisses were meant to last until you couldn't breathe... so why did his fist aim for her mouth instead? Why was I forced to block a hit when it should have been a perfect scene unraveling before my eyes and I should have been watching in awe because I pictured myself having that someday?

I thought that profanities were made for the bedroom and that pleasure was nice, but his venomous words dripped with poison, and it seemed like his horrendous satisfaction derived from our personal pain.

I thought that boys were supposed to mend hearts but instead he broke mine. Left it scarred. I want to know why he took the time to pick up my scattered pieces if his only intention was to drop them again? Why did he hug me tight enough for my body to feel safe and then let go as if I didn't just tell him that his arms felt like coming home?

Tell me, why did I think that love was some beautiful thing growing up when I never really knew what it was or how it worked? I always dreamed of lazy Sunday mornings and play fights that resulted in passion.

I always dreamed of feeling too much for someone
in the most pleasant and dangerous way.

My mother used to tell me that if you're going to
hold someone's heart, you must love it, too, but
what she forgot to tell me is that after you give them
yours, it's never guaranteed that they'll feel
responsible for protecting it just as you had with
theirs.

You'll become empty, numb.

And there's nothing worse than being alone at three
am with swollen eyes and a head full of thoughts
that repeat "How could you be convinced so
easily?"

do not fall in love with a sad girl.

we will entice you with our false smiles and feed
you with the thought that positivity is what's
running through our veins.

we will try so hard to keep ourselves from blowing
up over the tiniest things for in fear that if we do,
we will frighten you.

we will fall in love quickly, because we've never
been able to latch onto anything besides the
sadness, and the presence of a human is much more
comforting than the constant static ringing through
our ears.

we will open up slowly, forcing you to pry our lips
apart so we can tell you about our past, our
unhealthy habits, and whatever else we have kept
hidden for so long.

we will become infatuated with your existence and
want to speak to you as often as possible.

we will need a constant reminder that you haven't
given up on us yet, and that despite whatever
hardships are shot at us, you will still love us, bullet
and all.

we will force happiness even when our eyes are
overflowing and our fingers can't seem to stop

shaking; we will force happiness because we've been taught that boys don't fall in love with sad girls, and now that we have you, we are so fucking afraid of losing you.

we will overthink and overanalyze everything to the point where we're the ones causing the complications, not you.

we will push you away to see if you care enough to stay. it is a test; we will always feel obligated to test you in order to see how much uncertainty and confusion you can take.

we will say something cruel but not mean it because sometimes our emotions overpower our voice. and we'll apologize for our thoughts slipping out because that's not who we are. we are fragile, delicate. we need you to forgive us when our facade cracks.

we will break, shatter, become numb, inflict pain upon ourselves in hopes that one pain can rid the other.

we will falter, cry, become distant.

we will think that no one can ever love us again because of the aftermath of the destruction we have tried to clean up so many times before.

it's an endless cycle of temporary happiness and
permanent ache...

do not fall in love with a sad girl,

do not fall in love with a sad girl,

do not fall in love with me.

I write about love a lot because it's a topic that intrigues me.

It's interesting, the whole concept of it and what it's capable of creating and ultimately destroying.

I believe that love exists. I've seen it. I still see it.

I see it in the way that my grandmother talks about her deceased husband, and how even though he's been gone for almost fifteen years now, she is still madly in love with him. He took her love with him to the grave, and there's a sad, but hopeful, kind of feeling attached to that thought.

I've seen it in the way that couples hold hands while walking down the street, fingers intertwined so tightly for in fear that if they let go, they'll lose one another in the crowd.

I've seen it in the way that she can't seem to stop her gaze from fixating on the features of her lover, or the way that he rests his hand on his partner's thigh or wraps his arm around their waist, as if to inform everyone around them that they are theirs. People are not property, this I know, but there's some sort of relief, or safety, in the words "mine", "yours", "his", and "hers."

I've seen it in the way that anger turns into regret, and how regret turns into apologies, and how apologies turns into forgiveness, and how forgiveness turns into hugging, and how hugging turns into kissing, and how kissing turns into falling asleep in each other's arms, and how through all of that pointless bickering there was still the presence of love, it was just hidden somewhere in the walls, afraid that if it came out to intervene, it would get tangled up in the web of temporary hate.

In a way, there's something beautiful about an argument, and how two people are capable of overcoming it because the passion never left. The love never left. It shows that couples are willing to try and get through a hard time together because the world doesn't seem right without the one they are infatuated with in it.

I've seen it. I've seen love before. I've seen what it can do to someone.

And it's funny, you know? How most of us swear that we can love another human being with all that we have, but when it comes down to it, we are completely incapable of loving ourselves.

zero… a chubby little baby named alexa marie had been born.

two… i learned how to use the potty all on my own.

four… i wore floral dresses and dainty little shoes to a place where i felt welcomed.

six… i decided that i wanted to be a famous singer when i grew up.

eight… i had changed my mind. i wanted to be a professional soccer player instead.

ten… i had no trouble speaking up. i enjoyed meeting new people.

twelve… i couldn't wait to be a teenager.

thirteen… i kept dodging his kisses. i wasn't sure if i was afraid or if i just wasn't ready.

fourteen… i had moved on and took a chance, but all i got out of it were broken promises and a razor blade dangling at the end of his fingertips.

fifteen… i tried to be better, but i didn't know how to fix something so damaged.

sixteen… i feel trapped. lost, almost.

sixteen… i forget what the definition of normal is.

sixteen… they tell me to fake a smile and say that everything's okay, but how can i pretend that everything's okay when the world around me continues to move on while i'm stuck living in the past?

sixteen… i prefer the darkness.

sixteen… i am afraid to speak in fear that nothing i say is important enough.

sixteen… i cling to bad habits and let them drown me, even though i know how to stay afloat.

sixteen… i am alive even though sometimes i wish i wasn't.

sixteen… i have a whole world to explore and new memories to photograph.

sixteen… i am only sixteen.

sixteen… i am not okay. (today)

sixteen… i will be okay. (someday)

*author's note: i am now nineteen years old, and i'm okay.

*spoiler alert: you will be okay, too.

To the reader… today is going to rock or today is going to suck. You have some say in which direction your day goes.

Put on your favorite outfit, play with makeup, put on really bold lipstick, dress up for yourself, never for others.

Take too many pictures, laugh at nothing, take a hot bath, put bubbles in it, blast your music loud enough so your neighbors can hear it, try different genres of music, go outside and explore, by yourself or with a friend, collect some pretty leaves, find a forest or an open area and scream; scream until your lungs feel like they're going to burst.

Put on comfortable clothes and lie in a field of flowers, text an old friend, compliment a stranger, smile. Smile, smile, smile.

And breathe, take a deep breath and calm down, relax.

You're alive.

Today is just another day, yes, but it's your day. Make yourself happy today. Let the hours you have left mean something.

Take chances, take risks, live.

I love you, and everything will be okay. I promise.

I don't understand feelings.

How you could be so in love with someone one day and hate them the next?

How do full face smiles turn into unsatisfied frowns?

How does laughing turn into mockery?

I don't understand how we're capable of falling in love on a Saturday and falling out of it by Tuesday.

Most of our separations come with sorrow, they come with a feeling of guilt and hopelessness, a sense of "Where did we go wrong?" But hatred? That's odd. You loved them just the other day, right?

You were infatuated with the way they said your name at midnight and the way they kissed you in front of their friends - but now it's just embarrassing.

You can't stand it when they call you during their lunch break or when they hold on just a bit too long during an embrace you never even leaned into.

You anticipated the minutes counting down to when you'd see them again, but now? Now you pray for them to walk the other way when it's Monday morning and you pass each other on your way to work.

It's sad how our feelings towards someone are capable of changing faster than a light switch, how love and care can deteriorate into anger and shame.

I don't understand feelings.

I don't understand love.

After all, why take the risk if the outcome never changes?

Wouldn't you rather spare yourself the blade that others use against you and get scars from something that'll make you stronger, not weaker?

Life sucks.

Sometimes it really fucking sucks.

And you can replace the word 'sucks' with any other negative adjective and it would still make sense, but you can also replace the negativity with positivity, and I'll tell you this, that's a damn hard thing to do.

School has taught us that our grades are more important than our mental health.

Bullies have taught us that we're inferior to them, because we look different, because we act different, because we are different... or maybe they're just jealous (you know what everyone says, "they pick on you because they're jealous") but jealous of what? Is that really supposed to make the incident hurt just a little less?

Ex's have taught us that we're not good enough anymore, that we can no longer make their love thrive for us but instead make it dissipate as if our healed heart means nothing, as if a band aid can stop the ache in which we feel inside now that they have left us behind. But we can't really blame them, can we? I mean, come on, did you really think that your middle school love was going to be the only one you kissed for the rest of your life?

Mirrors have taught us to hate our reflection

because we no longer see ourselves, but rather the image in which everyone around us has tried stapling over top of who we really are - and it's a mess. An atrocious, saddening, uncleanable mess.

Society has taught us to compare ourselves and rip apart the question "What's wrong with me?" until there's nothing but tattered remains that we label as responses left.

"Because us girls don't have a thigh gap…"

"Because us boys don't have a six pack…"

"Because all of us as a whole don't exceed the expectations of perfection…"

But perfection doesn't exist. It is absolute bullshit.

You are going to feel awkward in your own skin, you are going to try and blend in rather than stick out, and you are going to fall apart. Okay?

You are going to fall apart, but that doesn't mean that you can't piece yourself back together again. It just takes time.

Life can suck most days, but this world is full of optimistic people, and if you cannot be one, at least try and find one, because maybe then you'll get a feel of what it's like to see life with your eyes open, rather than trudging through it with them shut.

When people distance themselves from us or completely leave us altogether, I think that it sets something off inside of us.

We blame ourselves for this because we think that it's our fault they no longer feel the same way towards us; we think that we said or did something wrong, which resulted in them giving us a final goodbye.

It's sad, because if you're like me, you don't just forget people. You don't forget the memories you made with them and how nice everything once was.

You begin to see them everywhere; you lace them in between song lyrics and plaster their face on the walls that surround you.

You hear the words "your fault" practically screaming at you from inside your head.

If you're like me, you don't just move on. You continue to hold onto to that sliver of hope that things will be okay, that things will be okay, that every broken promise and every harsh word that has been said will just disappear.

If you're like me, you give away five, six 'second' chances because you see the good in them while everyone else can't.

If you're like me, you love deeply, to the point where you give them your heart with the knowledge that they will break it. They will break it every time.

And if you're like me, you don't just stop thinking about them. You don't sleep for the fear of seeing them or hearing them in your dreams. You don't stop yourself from reading old text messages or listening to the voicemails that they left you when they went away on a business trip.

You don't become okay in a matter of a week, or a month, or even a fucking year.

If you're like me, you fall in love to the point where it destroys you, completely tears apart whatever morals you had, whatever vows you made to yourself.

And when you allow yourself to fall that hard, there is no chance in ever becoming fixed.

You will forever carry around the set of scars that have been carved from the one that you thought would save you from the darkness.

And isn't it ironic? How you called them your sunshine when all they ever did was carry a rain cloud over your head.

but there's something beautiful about him, and the
way that he can care too much or not at all.

the way he can spew out an overwhelming amount
of words or stay silent.

the way he can stand up for what he believes in or
fall down several times because a wave of sadness
has made a home in his veins.

the way his strength gives him the ability to
overcome anything.

the way he listens and understands and replies with
one-word answers.

the way he doesn't let his nightmares or bad habits
define him.

the way he's afraid of thunderstorms yet fits the
description of one so perfectly.

there's something different about him, and the way
that i know more than most people, yet i feel as
though i'll never know it all.

the way he's capable of hiding his feelings when
necessary and then bringing them back out when the
time is right.

the way we share moments that no one is ever going to know about because it's our own little secret, our own personal nighttime whispers that are so beautiful a novel couldn't even begin to explain it.

there's something tragic about him, and the way that his voice cracks in between sentences when he's talking about his past.

the way that i have to remind him to breathe when he wants nothing more than to just end it all.

there's something so mysterious about him, and the way that we don't make sense to not only ourselves, but to everyone else as well.

there's something calming about him, and the way that he finds comfort in a pen.

the way that he knows what he's doing in regard to situations that most people shut down in.

how selfless he is.

how curious he is.

the way he gets passionate when he's talking about a topic that sparks his interest.

there's something so addictive about this boy, and the way that even the mere thought of him keeps me up at night.

and there is something so, so beautiful about the way that he can love me with his whole heart when he swore to everyone around him that it has been completely hollow for years.

He's the kind of boy that girls fall in love with, and well, I guess I did.

Mornings were always the farthest thing from 'well slept', for I had slept only a fraction of the time I was given.

I spent my nights scribbling mindlessly on black napkins with blank ink because I knew that no matter how well my words were, they would never come close to what he was. I didn't think that it was fair for an abundance of metaphors to be seen when they were not written to their greatest extent.

He made my head dizzy in the best way.

This caused my poetry to falter in the best way.

The familiar scent of French Vanilla coffee always left a sweet trail from the kitchen to my bedroom door. It amazed me how fast I could finish a pot all on my own.

Showers became longer, for I always found myself thinking about the curve of his smile and how wonderful it would feel to stand under the running water with him... my head on his chest and his arms wrapped tightly around my waist.

My friends would often catch me daydreaming in class.

They'd call me later that night and ask if I was okay, to which I'd just smile into the receiver and tell them that I was thinking about music or something. I could hear them roll their eyes and laugh before hanging up, content that they'd figured out the reasoning behind my antics, but they'd never know the truth. So I'd put the phone back in its cradle, lay face down on the living room floor, and continue to imagine up a world where nothing but happiness exists; a world that consists of only him.

His name is so lovely. I often blush at the thought of being able to say it on a daily basis.

He intrigues me, and I think that I'm in love, or maybe it's just an infatuation that's bound to take a wrong turn.

All I know is that every time I hear him laugh, or watch him watch the world pass by, life doesn't seem so intolerable anymore.

It's like he went and took the sun right from the sky and injected its warmth into his skin, and I don't think that I've ever been so fond of the daytime until he became my only source of light.

i think i'm sad because i saw mother and father arguing when i was still too young to even comprehend what the words "fuck" and "hate" meant

i remember crying on the floor and being too weak to pick myself up

i remember acting as a shield for her so that she didn't become as black and blue as the bruise that i got on my knee from not being careful

i think i'm sad because i was happy for a while and one day the universe decided to give it to someone else

i should be grateful though right

i was allowed a few years of happiness and now it was someone else's turn to get it but why did i have to get sadness in exchange

why couldn't i just receive the feeling of being content

i think i'm sad because i loved a boy who loved another

i was forced to watch my best friend kiss him

forced to watch their love thrive while i pretended
that every laugh they shared and every hand hold
they had didn't feel like a punch to the face

i never understood the concept of love

i still don't

i think i'm sad because the boy i dated in eighth
grade broke up with me for a condition that i didn't
ask to have

i can't help it

it's not my fault

he taught me why promises can't be trusted and how
deadly a boy who says "i love you" too quickly
really is

i think i'm sad because when we have group
discussions in class i'm forced to talk quietly to
myself

i think i'm sad because everyone who promised to
stay has left and i was never prepared for that kind
of pain

i think i'm sad because my own reflection scares me
sometimes

i think i'm sad because four cups of coffee with
extra sugar isn't enough to get my brain to stop
thinking about destruction

i think i'm sad because my hand shakes at the mere
thought of being awake for another day

i think i'm sad because i see pretty girls on
magazine covers and commercials full of bones and
dainty wrists and i wonder why i don't look like
them

i think i'm sad because the moon has gotten tired of
hearing me cry and the stars no longer wish to shine
for me

and i think i'm sad because i prefer the comfort of a
graveyard rather than the comfort of my own skin

my own body

Smile today, even if it physically pains you to.

Put on comfy pajamas and stay in bed.

Make a cup of hot coffee or hot tea or any other beverage you prefer and sip it by a window; look at what's outside and admire it, no matter how vacant or fulfilled it is.

Listen to your favorite song on repeat until it bores you.

Listen to piano and violin covers and slam poetry; they're all so beautiful.

Take a hot bath with too many bubbles and hum a tune quietly to yourself.

Feel a sense of calmness today.

No loud noises, no distractions, no sadness.

Just feel a piece of serenity.

It's okay to feel a little short of happiness, but I don't want you to cry today. I don't want you to wish anything bad upon yourself... I don't want you to hurt yourself, okay?

Just breathe. Write even if you think you're bad at it.

Finish reading a novel, make really good food or order out, call a friend and talk about that cute boy or girl in your math class.

Smile, please.

The universe loves you. Your body loves you.

Take care of yourself today.

Every little thing is going to be okay, everything
will fall into place.

You are worth more than bad days and puffy eyes
and you must remember that this ache will pass, that
it will all be okay.

School has taught me that my grades are more important than my mental health, that on-time papers mean more than late night anxiety attacks for the fear of not writing my open-ended essay in the proper format.

School has taught me that sleep isn't necessary, that studying for four tests on four different subjects all in the same day will benefit me more than allowing my brain to take a rest.

School has taught me that in order to stay awake and get through the day I have to drink a 24-ounce coffee every morning and completely skip breakfast because god forbid I be five minutes late to class and have to walk in with my head down to avoid everyone's eyes.

School has taught me that I don't belong in a certain group, that despite all the taken seats in the cafeteria I will still get disgusted looks from the batch of popular girls when I try to sit near them.

School has taught me that no matter how hard I try to look my best it will never be good enough, but that's okay, right? Because the numbers on my report card will always reflect me better than my own personal choices. Besides, colleges don't care how much you paid for your shirt, why spend time obsessing over how you look when you can use that time to focus on how smart you're expected to come across as?

School has taught me that if I somehow gain the courage to raise my hand and answer the question I will most likely get over talked or told that what I have to say is not important enough.

School has taught me what it's like to have panic attacks in the bathroom, and breakdowns in the gym locker room, and pounding headaches in the hallways, and tired eyes during lectures, and aching hands while trying to scribble all the notes down before the teacher moves on. The list is infinite.

School has taught me that if I stutter while presenting or trip over my own two feet or even cough too loud I will get judged.

School has taught me that it is not, nor will it ever be, a welcoming environment.

I'm surrounded by kids that don't give a damn and it's scary how intimidating your own peers can be.

School has taught me that the word 'education' is bullshit.

We're all a part of this big memorization game, and I'm so fucking tired of losing.

Dear girl that falls in love with him next...

He's stubborn.

He'll focus on your words and take them into consideration but never quite leave them as just that; he'll let them linger for a bit but come back with a thought that really makes you think, despite how angry you may be at him.

When he drinks you're greeted with bubbly phrases or salty tears. He's never been one to play it safe so be careful when his whispers are slow and unsteady.

He will remember fragments from the previous night of alcohol and mixed emotions... watch what you say.

He'll remind you how to breathe again when you swear that every breath you had has already faded like the sunset he took several pictures of hours before.

He'll speak to you, calm you, listen to you, write about you.

His mind is so beautiful, never take his thoughts for granted.

He's afraid of thunderstorms, so comfort him when he hides under the covers and make him sing the ABC's with you as a distraction.

Love him.

Don't get offended when he throws harsh words at you because never for a second would he ever throw a fist at you, and don't be afraid to speak your mind, don't be afraid to tell him what you're thinking because he admires that, and you'll admire how strong his exterior is despite how fragile his interior is.

Be patient with him, he is a locked door. You can either find the key or break the door down, but either way, you will never unlock every part of him, and that is something you are going to have to accept.

His past resembles shattered glass mixed with torn photographs and memories that aren't always worth remembering.

Care for him. Tell him that you love him. Show him that you love him. Curse him out. Call him up at 3 am. Sing to him even if your voice is hoarse. Just love him, please. Do a better job than I did and never let him go. Someone like him is not worth losing over pointless bickering and faulty sentences.

Don't hurt him. Don't give up on him. Don't fucking leave him.

Love him, love him, love him.

I want you to cry.

Cry until your eyes burn and your sheets are filled with snot and tears.

Cry until your body's shaking and your head feels like it's on fire, then wipe your nose, drink a cold glass of water, put on calming music, and sleep.

Tomorrow will be better despite the puffy eyes and aching body, trust me, it will be better.

I want you to scream.

Scream until your throat is red and your voice gives out.

Scream until the air can't take it anymore and you're weak enough to collapse without even caring where you land.

Tomorrow your head will hurt, but you will feel okay, you will.

I want you to write.

Write until your hand is throbbing and your mind can't even form a logical sentence.

Write until the ink runs out and fill up all the pages
with the painful thoughts that keep you up at night.

Then crumple the paper, miss the trash can, get up,
and with all your force, throw it directly into the
bin.

Tomorrow you'll feel a bit empty, and that's okay.

I want you to go out.

Meet up with some friends and barely escape a
troublesome act.

Take pictures; capture the smiles and cherish the
night air.

Leave your current thoughts at an abandoned
alleyway and create new ones, happy ones.
Tomorrow you won't feel regret, I promise.

I want you to laugh.

Laugh until your cheeks hurt and you feel short of
breath.

Laugh until people start questioning what's funny,
then simply smile at them and say "nothing."
Tomorrow you'll feel proud of yourself for

attempting happiness, and even if it was false, it was still present, and you tried, and you'll feel so damn proud of yourself for trying.

I want you to relax.

Breathe.

It's okay to break down, it's okay to feel lost, and it's okay to not be yourself for a while.

You'll have off days and you'll forget who you're supposed to be.

You don't have to find yourself yet... you don't have to find yourself at all.

Instead, create yourself along the way.

Today is today and tomorrow is tomorrow.

Tomorrow always brings another opportunity, another chance, and today will be over before you know it.

So be bold, be brave, be confident, be daring, be loud, be you.

You are so beautiful, so loved.

Remember that.

i am a wildfire growing bigger and bigger with
every smoke-filled lung that tries to heave in as
much air as it can get

i am a lighthouse that can't guide you for i am
confused on where to turn

i am a broken windshield that is meant to protect
what's inside but instead i let them break me and i
watch as they take what i love the most

i am a raindrop that falls too fast the one that always
hits the ground the hardest while my friends just
watch and soon join me without decision

i am the tree that gets struck with lightning but
doesn't completely fall down

i can't stand on my own anymore and my god does
it hurt

i am the spilled accident on isle three that people
just step over while i wait for someone to care
enough to clean up what i can't

i am the frustrating pulse running through a vein
during times of confusion the pleasurable pulse
during times of sex the distraught pulse during
times of nightmare after effects

i am the text that can't send as if some unknown

force is giving you a second chance to redeem yourself

i am the scribble of words on lined paper at two am

i am the cracked mirror when a sight becomes worse than a thought

i am the hesitant string of curse words that you mutter under your breath for in fear that if you explode someone will label your stress as a condition that you do not suffer from

i am the pleasant darkness the terrifying sun the deafening silence the comforting noise

i am everywhere and i am in everything and i don't know if there is anything more satisfying than that

Yesterday I illegally crossed highways at 9:30 pm with two of my closest friends; I laughed a little too hard at Wendy's and bought a journal and a book on reasons to be happy at Barnes and Noble, and you know what? It was such a great fucking night.

Usually I just spend weekends at home in my room, but I'm learning how to go out more and enjoy the little moments in life.

I think that it's important to focus on what's around you, because one day it could be all gone, and you shouldn't dwell on people or events that hurt you but rather replace those bad memories with things that make you happy.

You can be happy, did you know that?

No one has the power to take that away from you unless you let them.

So go out and be rebellious. Wake up on the wrong side of the bed with messy hair and a few friends sprawled out on your living room floor.

Take lots of pictures and videos, but don't stay on

your phone too long, enjoy the outside world and enjoy the company that you're getting to share it with.

I know that life is hard and I know that things hurt sometimes, but you can't spend forever being sad.

At least try and make an effort to do something with your day, it feels a lot better than sitting inside watching the world find happiness while you claim to search for it even though you remain hidden behind locked doors and closed windows.

Go out and live. Get rid of the negative thoughts and smile.

And remember that you are a brilliant forest fire with the power to burn any asshole that tries to put you out.

He

Is the reason I can no longer sleep

For when I finally doze off

He's laced in my dreams

He

Is the comfort that haunts me at night

For such a daunting sound

Has never been so polite

He

Is the clock that ticks with force

For a mind like his

Surely needs no remorse

He

Is the wind that chills me so

For such a threatening laugh

Has never taken a blow

He

Is the whisper that calms me down

For a few shallow breaths

Are what keep me around

He

Is the dark that stems with fear

For an innocent like me

Has never seen so clear

He

Is the love that comes with lust

For I admire his everything

But I yearn for his touch

these tears are fucking acidic, for they burn on the way down

i've tried my hardest to rid the static, but it's still the clearest sound

my head is wrapped around darkness, please tell me what is wrong

there's a melancholy, bitter feeling, attached to this endless song

the voices get so loud at night, taunting me for what i've done

i'm trapped inside an endless tunnel, but my feet won't let me run

the air has become so heavy, swallowing me as a whole

is it bad that i don't really mind?

for i never wished to exist at all

maybe this is for the best, maybe i should just disappear

maybe i was meant to grow so tall, then be cut down soon after a year

Sometimes people are toxic.

They will poison you with camouflaged lies and entice you with ideas that intrigue you the most. They will bury their fears inside your head and push aside your thoughts as if they do not matter, just to get you to focus on their wellbeing rather than your own.

Be careful when they beg you to stay, it is a warning sign, and you will regret ever making that damn promise.

You'll begin to think that you deserve this: the constant guilt for something that you did not trigger, the everlasting episodes of breakdowns for the fear of not being good enough, the torturous silence when they don't call and decide to sleep on their own instead, the heavy heartaches during their times of disappearance, the lack of ability to speak up when you know for a fact that you are not in the wrong this time, and so on, the list extends for as long as you allow it to.

You will fall for them.

You will develop a certain safety in their two am whispers and random acts of kindness after a long, heated argument. You will become accustomed to their crooked smile and the way they must kiss you five times before saying goodnight. You will make up excuses for their absences and put in a good word when your friends ask how you guys are doing - but that is not enough. Your familiarity does not equal healthy. Your love will not always be reciprocated.

You cannot try and empty out a ten-foot pool of despair in hopes to fill it with two feet of temporary happiness, it does not work that way. It will never work that way, and you will only end up drowning.

Resist the urge to crawl back to them after they have said goodbye, because all that leaves you with is bruised knees and aching palms, and no one will feel bad for you. No one will clean up your mess.

You must let it end.

You must stop letting it hurt.

Remove the toxicity and allow yourself to grow on your own without depending so much on another human heart, for their heart screams trouble, and yours whispers hope, and you are the brightest flower in the field that doesn't deserve to get stepped on, but it will happen, again and again, and that is okay.

You will grow back every time.

You will sprout again, and you will become even stronger than you were before, even stronger than you ever thought possible.

from a young age

we endured what we thought

to be love

but a broken bottle

screams pain

and a fist

screams blood

and i thought that a

kiss was to signal affection

but his poisonous mouth

only shot out directions

and i don't think that it's fair

to pick a habit over a kid

for when you've

nowhere to turn

where does your mind plan to live

you've implanted an image

you've given them false hope

and what good is a parent

if all they give you is a home

a home is not stable

if you're not given any care

you can't expect them to grow

in an environment so unfair

you're not teaching them well

they'll pick up your mistakes

for daddy is their hero

and mommy makes things okay

but it isn't okay

how can it be

when your fathers out late

and you're watching him leave

and how is it okay

if you're seeing mother fall

she's stumbling all over

and you think it's your fault

but it isn't your fault

it never was

you didn't ask for the pain

all you wanted was love

and your mind is so scarred

from all that you've seen

but not every heart's degrading

for this is merely a horrid dream

and i know that your chest

has been aching for a while

but the stars that you talk to

just want to see you smile

and i know that every breath you take

feels like a wound

but a flower cannot grow

if you're impatient for it to bloom

I sat on the cold floor with my guitar in nothing but my underwear at one in the morning and sang to him in order to keep him calm while the air outside grew warm.
The thunder shook his fragile house and the lightning forced him to take shelter under the only small blanket that he had.

My voice was a low whisper and a shaky tone that cracked every now and then, but he still listened and he still smiled because he knew that it was his song and that the lyrics were written for him... only him.

When I finished I asked if it had helped at all and by the sound of his shallow breaths and quiet snores, I knew that it had worked. I was content and I was okay.

But today I am sitting on the cold floor in my underwear again and I can't help but sing his song so slowly and so gently, except this time he isn't on the other end of the line listening and there is no thunderstorm raging on outside of his bedroom window and I find it difficult to breathe. The words keep getting stuck in my throat and my chest keeps heaving and my eyes won't stop overflowing with debris from every memory that I continue to hold onto.

And today I am the one in need of a comforting voice, but the decision of his absence has already been made, and I never even had a choice.

i gravitate more towards a lonely soul because maybe if one half of the darkness connects with another half it'll mistakenly turn into light

and maybe if i cut out all the sorrow and pain that i feel inside of me i'll somehow be able to breathe their blackened heart back to life

maybe if i linger over the jagged lines and the dark bruises that are more noticeable than skin i'll be able to fix them up

and maybe if i kiss their broken bones then they'll finally feel like they're enough

maybe if i use my palms to lift them off the ground they'll be able to spread their wings and fly

and maybe if i hold their hand a little too tightly they won't be so hesitant to try

maybe if i invade their dreams and block out the nightmares then they'll finally be able to slow down and sleep

and maybe if i start to skip out on my own rest it won't be so bad because they'd be getting what they need

maybe if i focus on the wellbeing of others i'll be able to feel proud and like i'm doing something good, but maybe it's not so healthy to put a functioning heart before my own no matter how badly i believe that i should

Love is not found in cigarette ashes, not found in the bottom of a rusty flower vase, not found in lengthy text messages with enchanting words that make you stumble over your own thoughts.

Love is not found in the last drop of whiskey, not found under the welcome mat that has been stepped on by too many visitors, not found in the dark of the night while kisses shine brighter than the stars.

Love is not kept by throwing fists when things turn sour, not kept by shoving their belongings into a cardboard box, not kept by leaving the door unlocked in hopes that they'll let themselves back in, only to find their way back into your arms.

Love is not kept in between cement cracks and rusty promises, not kept in disappearances and heated jealousy, not kept in heart shaped boxes that no longer hold any value.

Love is not forgotten by deleting text messages and old pictures, not forgotten by blocking their number while trying to block out their face as well, not forgotten by fucking others in an attempt to get them the fuck out of your head.

Love is not disregarded by choking on smoke and drowning in your own tears, not disregarded by petty lies and overfilled notebooks, not disregarded until you learn to move on...

And you cannot move on until you learn to accept the fact that when the phone rings, it won't be their voice you're hearing on the other line.

You are allowed to let your fingers tremble while you grasp the edge of your shirt in hopes to slow the world down, but you are not allowed to let the earthquake inside of you ruin that pretty little smile of yours.

You are allowed to lock yourself in your room for a few minutes, hours, days even, if being alone will help you calm down, but you are not allowed to keep the key, you must give it to someone that will force you out of the darkness before it swallows you whole.

You are allowed to leave tear stains on your pillowcase if letting the debris spill from your eyes will help you see clearer, but you are not allowed to let the flood drown you; you must stay afloat.

You are allowed to take a walk in the wrong direction as long as you learn what kind of negativity lurks there; you cannot grow wiser if you never mess up, but you are not allowed to travel down the same path twice... you wouldn't want to stumble over your footprints again.

You are allowed to turn red, you don't always have to be blue, but you are not allowed to let this color bleed from a cut that you inflicted, only let it show by the way your face conforms to anger and your screams echo in the distance.

You are allowed to get lost when the world keeps pounding on you and you can't take the raging headache anymore.

You are allowed to imagine that something is chasing you if it will help you run faster.

You are allowed to fall down and pick up some scrapes and bruises with you when you get back up.

You are allowed to come in contact with yourself and look the other way.

You are allowed to say no when your demons ask you to join them; you don't have to be afraid, they can't hurt you unless you give them the power to.

And you are allowed to try different methods in an attempt to kill your sadness,

but you are not allowed to kill yourself.

every night i pray to something bigger than i am

begging them to get you the fuck out of my head

but you're still there

you're always there

and there's a constant cloud hovering over me

but instead of rain

it's a downpour of your voice and it mimics

every

fucking

thing

you used to say to me

and the things you now say to her

and it won't stop

i can't make it stop

i tried swallowing matches in an attempt to burn the

remains of you that i've stored in my heart

but the smoke lacked direction and made its way
into my eyes

but i'm used to it

because ever since you left i've never been able to
see clearly anyways

i finally pulled out the knife that you had left in my
back

but instead of aiming it at you

i aimed for my chest

and it pierced my heart

but i didn't really mind

i was in pain the second you said hello

and again when you said goodbye

i don't think something so broken will ever heal

i don't think something so dead is able to feel

i left the door open in case you decided to come back

it took months

but you did

and it was okay

and we were okay

and i wasn't upset with you

and you said you still loved me

and everything was okay

but i came home one night to find you in my bed with a ghost that looked a lot like me

why did she look like me

why did you leave me alone the next morning

why didn't you lock the door

please stop walking out on me then come back expecting more

If I'm sad, hold me.

Don't speak to me in conflicting words and slippery tongues, hold me.

Let your fingers dance along my back and please don't stop.

Don't question me. I will open up to you after I've calmed down. Pressure me and I will explode, but then I will drown you in apologies, because I never meant to hurt you. I would never hurt you.

I am a faulty construction, a blueprint with the absence of the most important piece.

So I fall down, and when I do, everyone around me hits the ground, too.

But I don't mean to, honest. I don't want to hurt anyone. I don't want to hurt you.

If I'm sad, please hold me.

Listen to my heartbeat and trace dizzy words along my thigh.

Know that I love you, and know that we will be okay.

Hold me always. Kiss me forever.

Just stay, stay, stay.

He was the sweetest sin...

I was the deadliest prayer.

Chains bounded him to the rusty walls and he kicked and kicked and kicked at the gravel.

His toes cried out in pain, but his mouth remained still.

Clocks worked feverishly, reminding him that the constant tick tick ticking of the hard-working hands were not what he should be fearing most.

Broken locks hung around his neck and he whistled loud enough for the birds to hear him, but they never whistled back.

He invited ghosts into his home when he should have been outside picking dandelions.

I cried every night, turning my bedroom into an ocean and letting my thoughts become the prey.

My father once told me to watch out for jellyfish when in deep water, but I became quite fond of them.

They caused me the pain that I desperately needed,

a certain sting to remind me that I was still alive.

They found happiness in the act of hurting me, so I let it keep happening, because who was I to deny a life lesson? Who was I to think that I deserved better?

Echoes bounced off the walls and dozens of shadows stumbled through the waves, enticing me with their performances so I never had any reason to leave my bed.

He was the sweetest sin...

Carefree and malignant.

His acts of violence never went unnoticed, but he didn't mind.

I was the deadliest prayer...

Choked up and vulnerable.

My screams of helplessness always went unnoticed, and I couldn't help but mind.

If someone makes a decision, it's on them.

It's their choice, and no one said that you had to follow their actions.

People change and things change and every little thing in this world changes every single day.

It is inevitable.

With every positive change comes a few negative aspects as well, and that is okay.

If someone is happy, let them be happy.

Let them make their own choices and if it's a bad one, let them learn from it.

No one owns you and no one controls you; you are in charge of what you do, what you say, how you act...

If what you're doing with your life makes you feel utterly happy, then keep doing what you're doing, because you must be doing something right.

If what you're doing with your life makes you feel sad or pessimistic, then change it.

You can do that; you are allowed to alter yourself in any way you choose in order to obtain happiness.

Fuck what people say, it doesn't define who you are.

And if you're the type of person to pick on someone else's flaws and put them down for their decisions, know that it's pathetic, and that hiding behind someone else's freedom does not make you free.

Maybe you should try fixing yourself instead of trying to fix someone who was never even broken in the first place.

Our love was broken bones and scraped knees on the playground after twelve pm. I trusted you enough to carry me home but you always stumbled just a bit too much; the blame was pinned on the fact that you couldn't sleep the night before, but I could smell the alcohol on your breath long before I even kissed you.

Our love was cigarette ashes and accidental burns. We'd count the stars and I'd always smoke consecutively. I choked and choked and choked but I didn't mind because for once, I finally felt something other than sadness. My head was light and airy, but your vile words always made me feel like a deadweight.

Our love was command after command and the occasional "I'm so sorry." I wasn't allowed to become friends with your enemies because you were insecure and I didn't want to lose you. I was blinded by the fact that your whispers were directed at me when they could have danced in the ears of someone else. You told me that you had a thing for chains and restriction and my god did you do a good job at tying me up and keeping me hostage.

Our love was alarm clocks and salty tears. I jumped at any opportunity to listen to your unsteady breathing and I would always catch myself smiling. You would hang up when I cried because you didn't feel like listening to my desperation and I thought that disregarding my pleads was okay. I guess you preferred your beauty sleep over my health, but even after eleven hours of being unconscious you still woke up with an ugly personality.

Our love was neglect and constant fear, uncertainty and miscommunication. "Oh my god I'm so sorry" and "Fuck off". "Baby I didn't mean it" and "You heartless fucking cunt". "I love you" and harsh names that melted into "Please don't leave me." "I'm over you already" and "Fuck you, fuck you, fuck you."

You were always so proud of yourself for getting me to stop hurting my skin, but I always found it ironic how my supposed savior was the one who triggered the majority of my harmful thoughts.

I fell in love with the devil, and I've never been fearful of fire until the day you proved that you were incapable of keeping your flames under control.

It's called depression.

It's called backing out on conversations because fear will always override potential friendships.

It's called constant trips to the pharmacy and swallowing more pills than food.

It's called "Sorry, never mind... " because if they didn't care enough to listen the first time then why the hell would they the second?

It's called midnight breakdowns and lack of sleep and wishing you don't wake up when you finally drift off.

It's called heavy eyelids and shaky fingers and self-talking breathing techniques.

It's called "I'm fine... " even when you want to rip your hair out and damage everything around you.

It's called multiple thunderstorms at once and the occasional hurricane.

It's called safe alternative lists and knowing that none of them will help.

It's called struggling no matter how hard you try to

recover recover

recover.

Such a simple word, but such a hard task to defeat.

It's called "Why are you sad?" "I don't know."

It's called deterioration of the mind and jagged thoughts that cloud your vision.

It's called tripping over your own two feet and crying because you thought that someone noticed. You think they're going to point it out, but they aren't.

It's called building up barriers and being so damn determined to not let anyone break them down.

It's called bitchy attitudes for no reason and pushing those closest to you away, and not even caring at this point to put in effort in hopes that they'll stay.

It's called depression.

It's called romanticized dark clouds and puddles of red, it's called kiss-the-scars-on-my-skin, it's called pathetic, it's called "Just be happy, stop being sad."

It's called chapped lips and being on bed rest for a week.

It's called "Oh my god, please make it stop."

We're told to appreciate our bodies, right? Told to love our bodies, right? Taught to take care of them because they are our home, right? Without a body, what are we?

We're told to embrace our scars and weird looking pinky, told to make friends with our stomach rolls when we sit down or bend over, told to be content with the way we are made... I mean, why should we alter what we're given? If we are born with the thought that original is beautiful, that our skin is our sanctum, then why is photoshop a thing? Why am I seeing before and after pictures of celebrities getting virtually slimmed down? Why does body shaming exist?

We all have fat, and there is absolutely nothing wrong with that.

You shouldn't be ashamed, okay?

You should be at peace with the reflection staring back at you because that is you, it's you. It's no one else, it's you.

Your butt freckle is cute, so is the way your thighs rub together when you walk.

Your chubby cheeks compliment your smile very well and your dainty wrists are absolutely lovely.

You are not the number on the scale nor are you the pair of jeans that you try to squeeze into. You are a personality, a voice, a hobby that you love, a song that you admire; you are so much more than an outer shell.

There is so much life breathing inside of you, so much optimism dancing around in there.

And I can only hope that none of you let the music end and allow the pessimism to take over.

my fingers reek of cigarette smoke and my clothes
leave a trail of regret behind them

you say you like it better when i'm bare but i can't
bear the thought of you touching me anymore

i've gotten used to sitting on rusty train tracks and
throwing rocks at inanimate objects but i can't bring
myself to become okay with the way you throw
yourself on top of me

you converse with my mother as if she were your
own but you play the part of your father every time
she turns around

you grab my wrist forcing me out the door while i'm
left to come up with excuses for the bruises
scattered all over my body

you just smirk at me and pull your lighter out of
your jeans laughing as if something were ever funny

sometimes when you're shoving alcohol down my
throat i wish it were your filthy words instead

that way instead of waking up hungover i'd wake up
embarrassed

i'd much rather feel small than feel the whole
fucking universe pounding on me inside of my head

when we drive down highways you put your hand
on my thigh and i tell you to keep your eyes on the
road

you've always been good at multitasking and it
makes me wonder how much practice you've had
despite you telling me that i'm your first

my hands shake with every step you take towards
me

you kiss me with chapped lips and the radio always
plays a bit too loud in the background

every time i turn the light off you become
vulnerable but then something snaps and you curse
at me until i turn it back on

i don't understand how someone so engulfed in
darkness could be so afraid of it

i hate sleeping naked because i don't wake up to
breakfast in bed instead i feel a cold hand on my
chest and i don't know how to make it stop

you spit out commands at me like you're training a
dog and i'm still trying to figure out how to break
the damn leash

you constantly bring the flame too close to my eyes
and i'm afraid that you'll be able to see the fear
behind them

you play with my hair gently when you're coming
down from a high and in that moment i can't help
but feel so fucking low

you tell me that i owe you everything i have left
inside of me

but i find it impossible to hand over an ocean of
emptiness

i tend to drink milk straight out of the carton when my mother isn't looking, and i often put two spoons in the freezer and let them sit overnight; i know that home remedies for sad eyes isn't a guaranteed success, but i'd much rather avoid their questions and keep my damn tears out of sight

my father likes to mention the fact that i'm getting older, as if i don't mark the calendar off every day; he says "honey, you know that i love you, but you can only rely on yourself when it comes time to pay"

i hear the expression "boys will be boys" a lot, and i find it a little peculiar how a slap to the arm means that they have a crush on you, so out of curiosity i read up on why a boy would leave bruises instead of love bites, and i think that adults sometimes confuse the words 'playful' and 'abuse'

my school has lunch time fairly early and that means that i'm usually not very hungry, but i try to swallow some food down anyway; i always hear the pretty girls talk about slim waists and big boobs, and i can't help but notice how their tummies shrink a little more every day isolation can come in many forms, and i usually feel it when i'm not alone; i feel it the most when i'm surrounded by noise, and i'm fucking drowning, but all people are worried about is answering their damn cellphone

I will break you.

Tear you apart until your insides meet the concrete while my eyes hold onto yours.

Kiss you violently, then push you away and confuse the fuck out of you until your head erupts like a volcano.

I will touch you gently.

Let my fingers rest on your thigh while you watch my hand.

You don't have to speak, I know what you want.

I will write your name down on paper only to throw it into the fire when I've run out of space.

The parallel lines look a lot like us...

close enough to touch but never meeting, never sleeping.

They just keep going and going and going, like the thoughts that you have about me whenever you're alone.

I will say goodnight with my lips, but I'm really saying goodbye when we kiss.

You think that I forget when it comes to taking my pills, but I always take too many instead.

I will blame my mood swings on the past and my anger on the alcohol.

I will talk like I know what I'm saying and stare at the sky while you stare at me.

I will constantly warn you about falling in love with a misplaced heart, but you'll just tell me that it would be an honor to find it.

If only you knew that I buried it somewhere deep enough inside of me that in order to grasp it, you'd have to hurt me first, and we both know that you're incapable of letting that happen.

The mere thought of scratching my surface makes you sick.

I will break your heart in the most confusing way, and I'll make you regret letting those three words spill from your mouth like the lies I whispered on your tongue the first night we got high.

I will break your heart because I cannot stand being heartbroken, and I don't know how to avoid a tornado unless I'm adding someone else's home to the damage.

i don't know what i'm doing or who i am or why the fuck i surround myself with teenage boys who see a girl's ass before they see her heart

and i don't know why i smoke too much when the taste of it makes me sick

and i don't know why i'm trying to kill my sadness when i swore to myself and everyone around me that i am so fucking happy

i am happy look i'm smiling so i must be happy right

i don't know why i walk on the railroad tracks instead of on the sidewalk or why i visit places that i'm not supposed to be at

i don't know why i sit on church steps and curse until i'm lightheaded like it's my own religion

i don't know why i choose something deadly to make me feel alive when i'm already living

i don't know why i take advantage of how white my teeth are or how my hands smell like lavender soap before i stain them with nicotine

i am so fucking confused when it comes to being me because i've lost her too many times already and i'm not so sure that she wants to come back anymore

and i don't know what i'm doing or what i'm saying
or who i'm touching or where my lips have been

and i constantly preach that i'm just doing this to
make me happy but if all this bullshit is making me
happy then why am i up at midnight lying to
everyone that asks if i'm okay

Stop thinking about them, because the truth is, they're probably not thinking about you.

They're either asleep or talking to someone else, and you've got to stop letting that get you down.

Stop sewing your mouth shut and forcing others to rip it open because all that leaves you with is blood and scars, and no one wants to listen to a train wreck.

Stop avoiding certain people and tell them straight up how you feel.

Brutal honesty is so much better than an easy lie.

When talking to someone, make sure you ask them how they are, too. It makes the person you're talking to feel pretty shitty when you only pay attention to your problems and not theirs as well.

Sometimes they won't want to open up, and that's okay, but trust me, just a simple, "How are you?" will make them feel like you actually care about them.

Most of the time they'll just assume that you're using them as a notebook when you've run out of paper, and that's a horrible way to think.

Stop feeling sorry for yourself, because no one feels sorry for you.

Most people won't pity you, but rather empathize with you, and that's a hell of a lot better than hearing "I feel so bad for them."

You've got to stop getting mad when things don't work out and feeling upset when the weather isn't bright.

You've got to stop digging up the past and learn to accept what's already been done.

You've got to stop biting your tongue, and scratching at your skin, and tugging on your sleeves, and taking two steps forward, but three steps back.

You've got to create your own happiness and fucking drown in it, because all you've got is yourself, all you'll ever have is yourself.

You have the loudest mind out there.

And everyone else?

They're just background noise.

Yes, I took my pills today.

No, I didn't skip breakfast again.

Of course I'll try to socialize with someone besides the teacher.

I know that people won't approach me if I keep my head down.

Please stop reminding me of my responsibilities, I know, I know, I know.

Mom, I promise I'm fine.

I like my piercings, Dad.

Grandma, there's nothing wrong with getting a tattoo.

I know that I can visit my aunt, uncle and cousins whenever I want. I know that they miss me, I miss them too, but you have to understand that I get nervous even around my own family members sometimes.

No, I'm not hiding anything, I just prefer sweaters.

Yes, I get changed in the bathroom for gym. I'm not

comfortable with my body being seen and seeing others as well.

Please just listen to me when I speak, for once just listen to what I have to say.

I get it, cursing isn't very lady like, but since when have I given a fuck if I'm acting proper or not?

Stop looking at me, I don't like eye contact.

I know, my fingers smell like cigarettes, no one said you had to like it.

I spend too long in the shower. I'm not revisiting old habits, I promise.

Trust me when I say that I'm trying.

Some days I just can't get out of bed, please don't force me to.

I get angry and bitter sometimes, just walk away,
we'll talk later.

My smile is crooked, but at least I can still fake it.

I know that I'm hollow inside, okay?

Please give me some time to fill myself up.

I don't want nor need your help.

Just let me figure this out on my own.

We were seven when you sang happy birthday to me all by yourself, holding a yellow balloon in your left hand and my pinky in your right.

The sky turned foggy, so we released the balloon and you accidentally let go of my finger.

You apologized after I slipped my hand back into my pocket.

You didn't mean to break your promise, and I knew that I could trust you.

We were eleven when you asked me if I wanted to go to the park with you and your family.

I tried to impress you by doing the monkey bars all by myself, but I landed on my stomach and your mother and father didn't seem to notice.

You rubbed my back gently and I realized that even after I had caught my breath, I couldn't help but lose it again when I looked at you.

We were fifteen when you started skipping class, so I started leaving notes in your locker during study hall.

They were filled with poetry about things that made you smile, because you said you liked how I could turn my thoughts into words, and I always told you how much I loved your smile, and how I'd do anything for it to show.

You grabbed my wrist softly after school and said "Stop worrying about me, I'm okay."

I tried not to worry, but you smelled like smoke and too much cologne and it was hard not to.

We were eighteen when you kissed me the night your car broke down.

I watched your eyes from the passenger seat and they seemed to lighten... from a dark sky to a calm ocean.

You put your hand on my thigh and said that you loved me.

We were sitting at that damn gas station for over two hours, but I couldn't bring myself to say it back.

I wanted to; you need to know that I wanted to.

We were twenty-one when our communication frayed and our adventures felt more like hospital visits.

You followed your dreams while I was still figuring mine out.

I never got to tell you how proud of you I was, or how I regretted not hugging you longer.

I didn't know that kissing you goodnight really translated to saying goodbye.

I didn't know that touching your chest meant feeling your heartbeat for the last time.

I didn't know that if had told you how in love with you I truly was, you might've stayed just a little longer.

Make sure you take your meds today even if you hate them.

Don't forget to eat a nice meal and smile even if it hurts.

Go outside for a bit and read or write or just enjoy your surroundings.

Text or call a friend and tell them how much you love and appreciate them (it's always a nice feeling to make someone else's day).

Play some calming music or have a rave in your bedroom by yourself.

Hug your parent or guardian and tell them something they're not used to hearing.

Take a hot bubble bath and try to think about positive scenarios.

Invite a friend over and paint or sing or take a walk; be productive.

Dress yourself up and take cute ass selfies and look in the mirror and realize that you are so beautiful, you really are.

Drink lots of water.

Let your anger out by punching a pillow.

Remember that it's okay cry.

Listen to the angel on your shoulder when it tells you that you are going to be okay. Disregard the little voice in your head that's trying to make you feel small just so it can feel bigger.

You have power, did you know that? You have the ability to say no when the world is pounding on you to say yes. You have the strength to turn around instead of jumping off the building.

Stop being afraid, stop worrying about other people's judgments because honestly, who cares?

They are not in control, you are.

Make memories, stay out past curfew, learn from your mistakes, do whatever the fuck you want as long as you're not hurting yourself or someone else in the process.

You got this, alright?

I wholeheartedly believe in you and I know that you can do this.

There is a world inside of you, okay?

But you have to give the world around you a chance, too.

Life is hard.

I'm expected to water my mother's garden twice a day and clean my father's shoes when he returns home from work.

My parents think that the gap between my bedroom and the front door should only take two minutes to reach one another, but I spend hours sitting on the top step wondering what would happen if the stairs disappeared.

They don't understand that in order to exit something, you must first enter it, and I've seen too many affairs come through the door at midnight.

My mother makes excuses and my father begs me not to tell.

They kiss in front of family photographs and I stare at the masks that they're both wearing.

I've been taught to sit with my legs crossed because that's what good girls are supposed to do, but lately

I've been stretching out and for once I don't care how improper my behavior is.

I was told that skirts are only appropriate when below the knee, but I've started to cut them short enough to reach my thigh and I don't mind the attention.

Sometimes when my mother isn't home I borrow her shirts.

Maybe if I expose myself like she does I'll be able to have a cheating husband and a one-night stand as well.

She always hoped that I would end up as successful as her and my god am I trying to be.

My father wears a tie even when he doesn't have a business meeting and I'm starting to think that it's used for more than just a fashion statement.

I never understood my parent's logic and how two cheaters can fall in and out of love so quickly.

Why set the table and cook dinner for three when you can eat out alone every night?

The whispers have gotten so loud that the house is starting to feel more like a high school lockdown and less like a home.

I started a fire in the kitchen in hopes that they would notice me, but they just laughed and put it out and then kissed each other as if the smoke wasn't hugging their lungs.

I went to my room that night with a headache and too much anger and now there's a dent in my wall, but they have yet to notice it.

Life is hard.

I'm constantly told to keep my head afloat and my body away from the waves, but you can fucking drown in a puddle if you really wanted to, and I'm beginning to think that I want to.

what once was is no longer more

for the day he walked out

i locked the door

and my benevolent dreams had distracted my fate

for one night i met a man

whose kindness shrunk by eight

drunken slurs and back handed hits

he was always proud

for he never did miss

i left a bloody trail from wound to rug

he would laugh bitterly

walk off and shrug

i tried to kiss my lips

for they didn't know another's feel

he'd rather hit my cheek

for i often lacked appeal

i slept on the ground

while he dreamt soundly in my bed

i thought

"how did this happen"

"why does he want me dead"

the answer cannot be pulled

from up above

for i've been through every rhythm and rhyme

the answer lives in his beastly soul

and i think i'm running out of time

bruises began to outline my throat

they started to resemble a necklace

people would say

"he's such a dear"

i'd say

"he's so fucking reckless"

sometimes i believe

that i'm able to change him

but you cannot help if they do not ask

sometimes people aren't always broken

just a little damaged by their past

and so

as a reminder

one you must never forget

a lesson that i learned on the way

if you feel guilty for the pain they have caused you

walk the fuck away

last night i got drunk because i was at a party and some guy kept telling me that i was pretty even though he had a girlfriend.

i laughed and it felt like i was spitting out bubbles instead of air.

the music got so loud that the house shook and the lyrics seemed to turn into drunken words and provocative body language.

the living room looked like a shitty museum rather than a sanctuary and every person's colors were spilling onto the shagged carpet.

a blurry painting submerged and it read,

"we are infinite, nothing can hurt us."

there was a vomit stain in the corner of the room but no one seemed to pay any mind to it; everyone just danced around it or added to it.

my hands were cold because it was late october and i was wearing something that my mom would never approve of, but the boys who usually passed me in the hallways took the time to talk to me and that was something i hadn't been used to.

upstairs the bed creaked and i matched the moans to a girl that i had class with in fifth grade; she was so loud that i started to wonder what i was missing out on, but i knew that my body was my body and i didn't want anyone to touch it yet.

i passed out on some girls lap at four am and woke up with a hand resting a little too far up on my thigh, but i couldn't figure out a name to go with the face.

i had to step over last night's painting on my way out and through dizzy eyes i noticed that it had grown; next to the previous set of words it read,

"we think we are infinite only when we are not sober."

too often it is told of me

to shut up when i barely speak

i'm encouraged to spit out wounded words

but when i do my mouth goes weak

and they'll say

"no one can hear you"

"come on try speaking up"

but no matter what volume i allow myself to reach

i've learned that it's never enough

i'm used to them telling me to get the hell away

to fuck off and leave them alone

but i don't think they understand

that a mind can't always be a home

and i've gotten used to the absence around me

i've befriended a frequent hum

"i don't need them"

"i don't need them"

but i often wish they would come

someone hung up posters last night

they read

"stop being depressed"

if only they knew that i'm trying so hard

but good enough isn't equivalent to best

too often ugly names are pinned upon me

but it's nothing i haven't heard before

so i'll just keep walking on broken glass

and hope that someday i'll be viewed as more

I think that life is bullshit in the sense of feeling too much when it's unnecessary and feeling nothing at all when it's very fucking necessary.

For example, I can't even finish a book without having my thoughts drift off because I can't go a few hours without thinking, "Wow, I'm a piece of shit and the popular kid that I have a crush on doesn't like me back because I'm not some preppy cheerleader that wears minimal clothing despite the weather and it doesn't take heavy eye contact to get me to fuck you."

I often hide at parties, and I don't get drunk enough to let my temptations overcome my boundaries, no matter how provoking they may be.

I'm a fucking queen, and I know damn well that I don't need a king to lust after my body only to leave when he gets bored of touching it.

I write about depressing shit even after I take my pills because I'm happy, and maybe that doesn't make any sense, but isn't that the beauty of it?

I love when people curse me out and tell me that what I'm doing is wrong, because I will not cry. I will not break.

I'm not here to please people. I'm here to please myself, and I will continue to do that until the day that I'm no longer able to.

I don't care if people walk out on me anymore; I anticipate it. I will willingly hold the door open for them and smile as they pass by. It's just one less problem that I have to worry about and I'm glad that they made the constant questioning come to a stop.

I don't believe in fighting fire with fire because all that creates is ashes and no one likes getting burned. I'll fight back with kindness and they'll laugh at me because they think that I'm too weak to retaliate, but I'm not, I never will be. I'm just smart enough to outsmart them.

I think that life is bullshit in the sense of feeling too much when it's unnecessary and feeling nothing at all when it's very fucking necessary, but that's why we're here.

Sometimes things don't work out.

You could die in two minutes or you could win the lottery.

You could fall in love or you could fall the fuck apart.

You could stay on the ground until the leaves bury you or you could pick yourself back up.

Learn how to make the days count, because nothing really matters if you're just counting down the days.

someday someone is going to wake up next to me, and the sheets will smell like coffee and my hands will feel too warm.

on the bedside table will be a notebook that's barely filled, because i'm not good at committing to journals but i'm not good at letting them go either.

i won't be wearing pants, only an oversized t shirt and a pair of lace underwear, preferably black.

i'll leave my slippers on the rug next to the mattress for when i have to get up, and i'll probably trip over them, but i'll just smile and laugh it off.

someday someone is going to wake up next to me, and i won't care how messy my hair is or how bad my breath smells, and they won't mind that i move too much in my sleep or that i feel the need to hold their thumb while i rest.

we'll just stare out the window and talk for hours on the balcony, and i'll write about them and they'll draw for me.

and they'll tell me that they keep falling, and i'll tell them that no matter what kind of falling they're doing, i'll always be at the bottom to catch them.

Everything is so fucking suffocating lately.

And when my mom asked if I took my pills today I told her that I did, because she didn't deserve to know that I had lost the bottle while searching for a reason to keep it.

And I've learned how to sleep with my back against the wall because there's too many clothes on my bed and I'm never home long enough to clean up the mess, but even when I am I still find a way to dance around it with excuses and I've become really good at dodging responsibilities.

The air that lingers from the front door to my mother's room smells a lot like cigarettes and heartbreak, and I can't stand coming home to see someone who I was told I would never see again.

I understand lies. I drown in them and there's no way around it when you speak to me so please don't fucking lie to me, because I am not oblivious, and I am not blind.

I'm not surrounded by innocence anymore but rather handcuffed to rules and lately I've gotten better at breaking them.

I've found a certain comfort in walking alone on the train tracks at night, and I always turn down the darkest streets because there's some sort of rush that comes with not knowing what or who's behind you, and sometimes I don't even care enough to know why the shadow behind me is not my own.

I keep calling people at the worst times and I can't help but delete my text messages before sending them because I figure that it's not worth sending... my problems are my own. I can handle it by myself. I can handle it by myself.

It seems like my body is so claustrophobic lately, and I'm not afraid of heights anymore but rather the outcome of falling.

I know that I laugh too loud and shut down too easily and I know that it's wrong of me to kiss when I'm drunk.

And I know that fire is dangerous and that the flames could swallow me up, but there's something that draws me to it and I find it impossible to try and threaten its passion.

And even when I'm late for school I still take my time coming in because no one really notices if I'm there or not.

And I know that I'm really fucking complicated and that my mind is a battlefield and that it loses too often, but for some reason I look both ways before crossing the street and I don't hurt myself like I used to, and maybe that's not enough for some people, but I think that it's enough for me.

I fell in love with bad habits at the age of fourteen because a boy fucked me over and I felt the need to take it out on my skin.

I saw pictures of cuts online and I thought that it wouldn't hurt to try it, but I became addicted to the pain and all it did was leave permanent marks that weren't always easy to hide.

Razor blades and rubber bands had become my best friends. My mom would question me about my sharpeners but I would just shrug it off and act like I wasn't up all night with a screwdriver and a head full of violent thoughts.

Melatonin nightmares took me away to a place that was dark and cold and I didn't know how to wake up. Sometimes I was afraid to wake up. Sometimes reality seemed worse than a bad dream.

Therapy sessions took up too much of my time and I didn't feel like talking anymore; I faked happiness and somehow it worked. I knew that it was wrong to lie but she was too blind to notice and I was too tired to care.

Time progressed and I felt lost without a path. No one bothered to search for me so I hung up my own "missing persons" posters that withered away before people could even read them.

I became obsessed with cigarettes because I hung out with people who needed them and I felt pressured to join in. I watched it burn more than actually smoking it and I couldn't help but let the ashes fall onto my wrist one too many times.

I started drinking at the age of sixteen because there was alcohol at the party and my friends encouraged me to try it. Sometimes it burned but other times it felt too fucking good. The idea of being light and airy always appealed to me more than being burdened with negative thoughts.

I fell in love with bad habits before the age of seventeen because sexting made me feel important and like I was capable of making someone feel good without having to completely reciprocate it. Spitting out dirty words always made me feel so guilty and for some reason I liked the rush.

I fell in love with bad habits because I was never surrounded by healthy ones growing up.

I've gotten used to destroying my body and not caring how intimidating or unresponsive I was, how distant and cold I've become.

And I can't remember ever painting a rainbow when I was younger but rather drawing dark clouds. And maybe that's sad, but maybe that's the way it was meant to be.

At age eleven I had my first kiss with a boy who
tasted like cotton candy.

His lips were blue and his eyes were green.

He smelled like an overpriced carnival mixed with
too much adrenaline, but that didn't stop us from
holding hands on the top of the Ferris wheel.

When I turned thirteen I kissed a boy who tasted
like mints and nervousness.

We stood by my friend's trashcan after our
conversation had dimmed because I was too
embarrassed to leave.

He smelled of bike tires and too much cologne, but
I thought that that was how seventh grade
relationships were supposed to be.

Sixteen turned into make out sessions rather than
quick pecks.

We sat on an unfamiliar sidewalk and his lips tasted
like cigarettes and caffeine.

The scent of used penny boards and sweat
surrounded him when he walked, but that didn't stop

us from falling asleep on the side of my house at one am.

When I turned eighteen I learned what making out led to.

His tongue tasted like alcohol and curse words and his attitude reeked of desperation and cockiness, but I thought that that was normal.

We fucked so hard and he didn't even kiss me in between moans, and every time I hooked up with someone different, I knew that they weren't going to kiss me like the boys did when I was younger.

At age twenty-two I met a man in the park who wanted to hold my hand.

His fingers felt like feathers and he smelled of ink and business.

We talked for hours until the air threatened us to leave and he invited me back to his place.

But instead of taking me to the bedroom, he took me to the balcony.

Instead of touching me, he looked at me.

And instead of fucking me, he kissed me.

He kissed me.

And that is so important.

It's so cold here.

The teacher keeps telling me that smiling is good for me but my lips stay pressed.

Students throw whispers across the room and I can't help but get tangled in them.

They don't concern me, but I've grown fond of listening.

The brunette in the front is "…having a party on Friday, parents are out of town, it's gonna be a banger…"

The kid in the back got laid by "…a freshman last week, it definitely wasn't her first time…"

One of the popular boys "…got a mustang for my birthday; it's nicer than most people's houses…"

It's all noise, too much noise.

Words are simply criminals let loose and no one cares if it results in death.

The hallways feel like a movie scene, the crowded sidewalks of New York.

There's make out sessions against the lockers and not enough time nor space to take a breath.

I keep getting trampled on.

I keep losing my balance.

I refuse to lift my head.

Everyone is so focused on where they are going and no one gives a damn if they hurt you in the process.

My notebook understands more than I do but my headaches keep getting in the way.

I raise my hand too often but I put it back down because I feel stupid.

I feel stupid.

I don't want to feel stupid.

I'm not dumb, I know I'm smart, but all knowledge leaves me when I walk into the classroom and I'm not quite sure why.

It's so empty here.

The desks are filled but the room is drained of individuality.

Transparency is evident in everyone, but I don't want to look anymore.

I know what they are made of: drugs, alcohol, stories of sex and mistakes, late night parties and fear. So much fear.

Young does not mean infinite, and infinite does not always mean forever.

Voices blend into one and I can't stop myself from trying to pick apart their sentences.

Fragments into completion, lack of personality into some sort of substance, boredom into entertainment.

I've learned that my peers keep me around because I am a fire starter, but once they light up, I no longer serve any purpose; they don't need the extra baggage.

I burn so often that my fingertips have begun to char my homework and it's not an excuse, it won't happen again.

It won't happen again.

I'm so tired, and it's so cold here, and everyone is a ghost.

We have grown and we have died.

We shed our elementary school skin and transformed into deadly high schoolers.

And I touched the building with a gentle hand on my way out, but all I got in return was a slap to the face saying,

"This? This is reality; learn how to deal with it."

One thing I've learned while being overly depressive and restless is that no one likes being around a sad person.

People can only take so much of your negativity before they begin to feel the effects of it, too, and the rumble of another's earthquake is enough to make anyone flee the scene.

Your thoughts are valid, yes, but they are yours.

No one can change the way you think when you've been thinking a certain way for too long, and you cannot possibly become angry at someone for trying to understand your mess, for trying to clean it up.

You have to stop drowning in your own self-pity because in reality, no one is going to jump in after you.

No one likes being around a sad person, and everyone knows that being happy is a difficult task, but the outcome of an event or a mood or even a mistake lies in your hands, and only you have the power to flip the switch and allow yourself to feel any other emotion besides sadness.

No one likes being around a sad person, okay?

And I understand how that statement may be harsh, but it's the truth.

You have to realize that no one is going to stick around if you keep getting lost in your own maze.

I found my beginning when I reached the end.

The book itself was never appealing to one's eyes, but for some reason I was oddly attracted to the destruction of the design.

Page numbers were missing and the words were smeared, but I became obsessed with the nurture that it needed.

I claimed my spot between the slow beginning and the treacherous middle and the manipulative end.

I was the whole god damn book, wasn't I?

I let someone else write out my life, let them control me like I was a script out of a movie scene, but I didn't know who held the pen.

My smile was smothered whenever I decided to take a break from reading such a black and white story.

I could only bear so much heartbreak, only endure so much pain.

I had too many altercations with myself but the writer would never let me change a thing; she said that it would ruin the plot.

She listened to me but soon laughed as if my despair was comical, as if my misfortunes were just fuel for inspiration.

I kept finding ashes in the crevices and coffee stains that didn't smell too sweet.

The folded down corners were supposed to be revisited but no one ever took a second look.

Most people didn't bother to finish reading the dialogue the first time.

I found my beginning when I reached the end.

I grew out of disastrous themes and characters that never showed any affection.

I gave up on setting fire to my hands and letting the enemy get the last laugh.

I had another talk with the writer, and her face looked a lot like mine.

I was too blind and naive. Too arrogant to be wrong.

Too stubborn to believe that I had any control at all.

I found my beginning when I reached the end, for I was finally strong enough to realize that one life does not equal one book, but rather an infinite amount of short stories.

I'm not comfortable with my body.

I hate the way my stomach looks when I bend over and I'm used to constantly pulling my pants up high enough to cover the bit of fat that shows whenever I sit down.

I have a hard time wearing tank tops and short sleeves because I don't like the way my arms jiggle when they move.

I get very self-conscious when someone looks at me too long because I manage to convince myself that they're picking out my flaws, but for all I know they could be thinking "that girl is beautiful."

The truth is we all have some insecurity that holds us back, whether it be skipping a party because you feel unattractive in every outfit you try on or it be wearing sweat pants for a week because you can't stand the size of your thighs... we all go through this.

I guarantee that at some point in your life someone has pointed out something about your body that you never even took notice of, and you can't let their sudden realization capture all your attention.

Some people say things out of spite, and although it's uncalled for, it still happens, and you just gotta learn how to smile and not let their words leave indentations on the way you perceive yourself.

Your skin is beautiful no matter what color it is. Your skin is beautiful no matter how scarred or tainted it is, and someday someone is going to love the person that lives beneath it... I hope that you can learn to love that person, too.

You are beautiful, and everything that you hate about yourself, someone else admires.

Stop being an enemy to your body, it just wants to be your friend. Stop locking yourself out when you know you'll have to come back in.

Teenage alcoholics.

God damn music turned up so loud that no one heard the mirror shatter.

Someone was mad, I think.

Curse words are so beautiful to the drunken ear.

Concoctions take place in the kitchen but they're fucking on the countertop.

Sober, I'm sober.

I'm watching my friend because a senior offered her rum.

She downed hers and she drank mine, too.

She's giggly and aggressive.

Courageous and loud.

Sober, I'm sober.

The air was bitter; the music was tasteless.

His steps were slow and he wandered too far.

I followed close behind him.

He cried because he meant no harm and I let him
pull me closer.

Calloused fingers roamed gracefully; I'd never been
touched like that before.

Last night of December, beginning of January.

My dress was chosen in the dark.

He kissed me and I let him.

Sober, I'm still sober.

Watching everyone gets boring.

Like a movie on repeat.

You know the dialogue.

You know the characters.

It's all for show, there's no real emotion.

I wanted to use the bathroom.

He pulled me down onto the couch and I was worried about my dress rising.

I was so dizzy and he took it the wrong way.

I only wanted to relax, try and make the world stop spinning until I could sense the ground beneath my feet again.

He tried feeling me up... everyone watched.

My head hurt and I pushed him off of me.

Thoughts turned into whispers and whispers turned into actions and I swore that I could hear the rain hitting the roof.

I wasn't sober but I was still conscious of what was going on around me.

I lost my hair tie and I reeked of other's desperation.

Home, I wanted to go home.

Smoking cigarettes behind bushes and inappropriate behavior and forcing yourself to man the fuck up and down whatever beverage was given to you.

Teenage alcoholics.

God damn music turned up so loud that no one heard the mirror shatter.

My knuckles began to bruise.

I just watched the blood stain the floor.

i don't know what the fuck i'm looking at.

these eyes aren't green, they're grey.

do you see that?

they're grey.

this smile is a result of an epidemic.

we're all sick.

the scar on my left cheek is a reminder, a precise
calendar moment.

stop listening to the mirror, it lies, but so do you.

so do you and you like that, don't you?

honesty is a precarious motion, a whimsical
falsification tied down down down.

down down down onto the bed.

children tend to grow up hating restriction and force

but somehow flourish into loving it when they reach that age.

the age of rebellion and negative demeanor.

i don't know who the fuck i'm talking to.

this boy likes me and it's bullshit.

i inhale toxicity in hopes of becoming fuller.

i try to exhale my predominant feelings but they're so fucking stubborn.

these eyes aren't green, they're black.

they're black.

stop telling me that such a delicate name should never be paired with such a dismantled figure.

i didn't ask for this.

my thoughts are unorganized.

the clutter is concerning and people get mad when i

refuse their entrance but flee when i give in.

let me drown in the waves of past lover's
fingertips... let me feel the scars I have left
behind...

let me read them like a blind person reads braille...

unorthodox nightmares.

there's no way to sugarcoat that.

i don't know what the fuck i'm looking at.

i'm aware of the rotting artwork that hangs
forcefully on my walls, but i never look at myself
long enough to realize that the decaying on the
inside tends to expose its smell on the outside as
well.

and i'm not a bouquet of roses anymore but rather a
corpse. i'm colder than a corpse.

why doesn't that frighten me?

why the fuck doesn't that make me want to change?

The last time I cried it was a Friday.

Monday morning was shattered by Sunday afternoon's conversations and Saturday night's regrets were triggered by Friday's actions.

You see, I don't know what I'm doing.

By Wednesday things seemed to calm down, but for some reason the walls around me remained grey and Thursday after school I walked home in the rain.

The stop signs disappeared and the puddles distorted everything around me.

My shower ran cold for three days and the sound on the television was never loud enough to hear.

My fingers pressed the volume button but all I did was break the remote.

Distance was no longer a thousand miles away but rather the amount of footsteps it took me to get from the front door to my bedroom.

You see, I forgot what it's like to not mess up.

When something breaks, usually someone throws away the remains, but there's been shards of glass in the center of my room for weeks now and it's a constant battle between wasting band aids on something I can prevent or owning up to what I've done.

The picture that was inside the frame is still missing.

It hurts too much to look for it.

Water bottles in the fridge have been drained and it's hard to keep my eyes open in public.

People think that I'm just tired but really I'm drowning and it burns.

It burns.

It feels good.

It feels good.

It makes me feel like I can jump from one building to the next without having to look down.

Look up, they keep telling me.

Look up.

The last time I cried it was a Friday.

They left me all alone.

They didn't come back for me, either.

You see, I don't know if I'm making the right choices or not, all I know is that I'm making irrational decisions at very chaotic and dangerous times, and somehow I've convinced myself that it isn't so bad to figure out how to fix the outcome after the damage has already been done.

Somehow I've convinced myself that in order to learn a lesson, you must experience something that you'd never let yourself revisit.

i can't tell you to stop hurting me

when i'm the one that's allowing you to

i invited you over at midnight

and for some reason you didn't refuse

four teenagers on two different couches

in a dark and quiet room

picture frames and artwork surrounded us

but i only looked at you

i didn't want to kiss you first

but god did i want you to kiss me

guilt seems to build up so fucking fast

and it's impossible to make it leave

2:30 am and we were still awake

while our friends passed out on the floor

fuck i'm surprised we didn't wake them up

when my back hit the bathroom door

the room was too quiet

and my head was so loud

i could've sworn you heard my thoughts

"fuck him"

"kiss him"

"hate him"

"miss him"

it's agonizing when you can't make it stop

the air was thick with lust and passion

a deadly combination every time

you loved me only when your hands felt skin

but left when my heart made a sign

i'll break your heart before i ever even let you touch mine and you'll be fine

you know you trust me

you trust me don't you?

fingerprints feel better than sheets

and lies taste sweet

and i've warned you before

a girl in pain is as dangerous as a storm

let her eyes blind you and let her voice be your downpour

look at me and tell me that you're strong enough to leave

even though we both know that i'm the only strength you'll ever need

the bedroom door remains open some nights

but you still wake up in my room

does being alone terrify you

or are you just too addicted to move

i'll try really hard to talk to you

but you mustn't let me in

i'll break your heart before i ever even let you touch
mine because oh my god

don't i deserve to win?

I keep shoving the idea of love so far down my throat that I puke every time someone tries to get inside my head.

My therapist thinks that I'm purging again, but I just want the indecisiveness to stop.

On Tuesday morning I ran into the boy that texts me every day even though I have yet to reply to a single message. He looked at me and said "Hey, are you busy after school?" To which I replied, "No, I mean yes, I have plans already." I've never been good at lying, but I sure as hell know how to make someone feel unimportant.

He just said okay and walked away.

I threw up at the nurse's office five minutes later.

In the middle of the mall parking lot my friends and I met some guys that carried around packs instead of shopping bags.

Being the most social of the group, I said yes when the skinny one asked if it was okay to sit down.

He offered me a cigarette and I found it difficult to say no.

A mixture of smoke and sickness made itself present when I spoke.

My friends wanted to leave but I wanted to fall in love.

Within two days I had learned that parking lots are not castles and boys with bad habits will never become your prince.

It was summertime and I didn't have to be home until eleven.

He regrets not kissing me; he still tells me that whenever we talk.

The stars covered us like a blanket and the scene was perfect, but I started getting nervous when he moved his body closer to mine.

I ended up excusing myself from the bridge that we were laying on.

He asked me if I was okay, if he did something wrong.

I said that I was fine, that he did everything right, but I threw up anyway.

Sometimes the heartbeat next to yours makes you

feel like coming home and it scares the hell out of you when you realize that.

I keep swallowing the idea of love in hopes to become so full of it that people will feel the need to touch me in order to become less cold.

My therapist thinks that I'm binging again.

When I was six years old my father told my mother that he loved her after he had hurt her.

He kissed her with the back of his hand and I grew up thinking that that was what affection looked like.

I've learned that the act of loving someone can kill you, or them, or both of you at the same time.

But most people seem to realize that only after it's too late... when there's nothing left to fix it, when words are not enough, when actions are not enough, when the headstones have already been engraved.

Empty fucking bathtub.

You think you're drowning, right?

Don't fall for that shit.

You can't drown if you never fell in.

I can hear your heartbeat through the walls.

You're sitting there with your head in your hands and someone knocks on the bathroom door.

Stop ignoring them, let yourself leave instead of forcing yourself to stay.

You're not real.

Look around you, nothing's real.

Inanimate people surrounded by devices that turn us into addicts.

Waking up with a hangover doesn't mean that you wanted to die last night, just means that you had too much fun.

Or maybe you wanted to create new fuck ups in an

attempt to cover up the old ones, maybe it all means the same thing.

You've flooded the bathroom with your thoughts because no other room in the house feels like home anymore.

You can't find your bed and even the couch doesn't want the weight of your recklessness.

Your mother's been asleep for days but you don't bother to check on her.

Your reassurance comes from the refrigerator light at midnight when she thinks she's the only one awake.

Your father said he was going out of town for two weeks but it's been a month.

You don't call him and he doesn't care enough to call you.

Your brothers getting high in his bedroom with people you've never met.

He's nineteen, you're not allowed to tell him that
you love him when his friends are there.

Your sister's been hanging around with your
neighbor too often for it to be quick conversation.

He's twice her age and she leaves the house in jeans
but comes home wearing skirts that are tight enough
to send the wrong kind of message if she bends
over.

Empty fucking bathtub, right?

You want to drown but your fingers are numb.

Turn on the faucet and let the water run.

Your thoughts bounce off the walls, forcing you to
inhale them again and again.

Stop being cold, let yourself float.

Drown in the gentleness that you've never felt
before.

Empty fucking bathtub when the house is sound
asleep, flooded bathroom floor when the first alarm
clock beeps.

he wanted to fuck me. said he could take it slow.
said he could treat me like a princess and make me
feel beautiful. it was one am and he was drunk.
thought he meant it, you know? but drunken words
aren't always sober thoughts, just spur of the
moment bullshit that naïve teenage girls believe.
sometimes lessons have to be learned the hard way.

i lied to my mom again. wasn't proud of it, but it
had to be done. she wouldn't understand. being
around guys more often than girls doesn't make you
a slut, just means that you know who your real
friends are despite society's judgmental tendencies.

she cut me off. can't blame her though. a person can
only fuck up so much before people get tired of
their shit. it was an accident, you know? at the
moment i thought it was what i wanted, but trying
to gain the attention of one isn't worth losing the
affection of many.

i can't help but stay cold. distant is how i like it. no
one can hear my thoughts. no one can touch me.

stop telling me that you know me. how can you

know me when i don't even know me? i don't know
who i am.

he wanted to fuck me. said he could make it rough.
said he could make me forget about everything.
fucking said i could trust him.

look at me, i've become toxic. addicted to bad
habits. in love with madness.

look at me, i've turned heartless. i can't even look at
myself in the mirror for more than two seconds
anymore.

please, look at me, and tell me that not all
reflections are seen the same through different
eyes.

tell me that someone out there can still see the good
that's left in me.

i don't like romantic.

i don't want first dates that end up in small talk and awkward hugs goodbye.

kiss me if you want me, but just because i kiss you back doesn't mean that i want you, too.

i don't date.

labels scare the hell out of me and i refuse to put myself in a position that i'm uncomfortable in.

i don't want late night phone calls with someone that i'm learning to love, i'd rather get nine hours of sleep than wake up to my phone telling me that the call ended three hours before i was supposed to get up.

paranoia seems to follow me everywhere i go, i don't need to fill my head with fear when your absence extends beyond the usual.

i don't feel sympathy for anyone; it's not my fault if you cry.

i don't want to fall in love, okay?

i don't want to fall in love.

all i know is flirtatious actions and dominant motives.

i don't want to share secrets with someone else because the whole world is one big gossip group and everybody's mistakes seem to line the walls of dirty bathroom stalls.

my feelings come and go; i'll tell you that i want you on saturday but distance myself from you by monday.

i won't let myself go down that path again, okay?

i'd rather be pinned beneath heavy breathing and dark eyes than be trapped underneath the weight of "forever? always."

i'll warn you not to fall in love with me, but you will, and i'll apologize even though i feel nothing.

i'm sorry. i'm so sorry.

i don't know what else to say.

We fogged up the windows in the back seat of his car on a Thursday night.

On the ride home we decided not to tell.

We know that mistakes often lead to consequences and both of us have already dealt with too much loss to be honest with certain people again.

By Friday morning he forgets my name; I forget his too.

Vacant stares across the room land hopelessly on each other's eyes.

The weekend holds expectations that often lead to disappointment, but sometimes a reality can become greater than a fantasy.

Friends can fuck, can't they?

We don't talk about what happened, not to anyone, not to each other.

By Monday afternoon he drives past me while I go back to my routine of walking home, pretending that I didn't feel his heartbeat jump out of his chest just a few nights ago.

We fogged up the windows in the back seat of his car on a Thursday evening.

I still remember the way he moaned my name.

"Pleasure is a part of life," he said, and I replied by letting my hand slide down to the hem of his shirt until his breathing faltered.

We kissed, we touched, we fucked.

We fucked so hard that two weeks later my hand print was still visible on the glass.

she broke his heart at midnight over the phone

said she wasn't feeling it anymore

said she never was

she's in it for the pleasure

doesn't care about what he wants in the long run

her mind is in constant motion

never really thinking about the last person she

touched

don't get attached

she warned you

said not to fall in love with her because she won't

catch you

she never will

you'll drown in the brown and green swirl of her

eyes

and the words that she whispers when she's

touching you from the passenger seat

you'll regret opening up to her because she'll never

do the same

she'll encourage you to continue even when she's

not listening

stop trying to figure her out

it's impossible to read someone that never wanted to

be labeled as a novel in the first place

you'll only find yourself getting stuck in between

frustration and confusion

and she'll move on in a few days

maybe a few weeks

she'll swallow your heart in hopes that maybe the

beating of another's will inspire her own to come

alive again

she won't love you

she can't love you

you're nothing but an afternoon daydream that got

caught in her nightmare and you need to wake up

wake up

stop being stubborn

don't be weak

she'll make you feel good

make you feel wanted

touch you until you're begging

she knows what she's doing

always has

you can't change what she's used to

and she broke his heart at midnight over the phone

got drunk two hours later and hooked up with a guy

that reeked of piss and smoke

fucked in a dirty bathroom stall

left him there

she'll break your heart

she will

and if she doesn't then you must be colder than she

is

and she can't stand competition

she'll mess with your emotions

you've just gotta figure out how to mess with hers

too

i can still feel his lips on mine, they are so warm
and inviting

the soft roll of his hips on top of me, pinning me
down until i drown in a sea of lust

"you're beautiful" he says

and i can't help but become embarrassed, because i
cannot see what he sees

"your body is beautiful" he says

and i kiss him, because no amount of words could
possibly compare to the thoughts that take refuge on
his tongue

i am content with his rough fingers dancing along
my thigh because he is here and i am here and there
is nothing around us that is forcing us to end our
infinite moment we call intimacy

but what i fear most is what comes tomorrow

because what if by tomorrow he decides that a girl who cannot love herself is not worthy of being loved

what if he decides that a girl who cannot believe a single compliment should not have the privilege of receiving many

Being a girl meant swallowing down every derogatory comment that was spit at us whenever we passed a man on the street.

"Hey sexy, why don't you come on over so we can have a little fun?"

And he would look us up and down and wink, and we would feel the vile taste of his words sneak back up into our throats and use it as a motive to walk faster, fearing that a man with such a dirty mouth would touch our clean body with his filthy hands.

Being a girl meant getting told no when we asked to play with the boys at recess.

"This is a boy's sport, you can't handle it."

And we would go home that night and practice for hours, only to come to school the next day and still get told no despite our capabilities. Stop saying that we

"Hit like a girl…"

Most of the time we hit it farther than you boys can.

Being a girl meant bleeding through our jeans on a Tuesday because we weren't expecting our periods to come until Thursday.

The green plastic seat changes color and our pants are stained red. The kids around us laugh and point. They say

"Hey! Guess it's that time of the month."

And we don't come to class the next day because a natural-female-accidental-occurrence is too much for a group of sixteen-year-old boys to handle.

Being a girl meant shopping for clothes that were too small for us because loose fitting shirts made us look boyish.

"No one will find you attractive if you dress like that."

And so we'd spend $200 on dresses, frilly shirts and high waisted jeans just to feel uncomfortable in them as soon as we put them on. Us girls shouldn't have to question our originality every fucking time we pass a reflective surface.

Being a girl means that there is a ban on cursing because profanity dripping from our pretty little lips is not considered ladylike.

Being a girl means being objectified because our bodies are portrayed half naked on billboards and magazines while our bra straps are frowned upon in school.

Being a girl means being told to wait for our prince to come save us when we know damn well that we can save ourselves.

Being a girl meant swallowing every derogatory comment that was spit at us whenever we passed a male on the street.

But we kept it down,

we never once threw up,

we fucking took it like a man.

I haven't talked to my dad in over three months.

My mom keeps saying that it's okay, that if he wanted to talk to me then he would initiate the conversation, but I cry myself to sleep sometimes and maybe he does, too.

It's been so long that I've forgotten what his voice sounds like and I don't even remember his phone number anymore; I don't think that he remembers mine, either.

My siblings keep aging faster than I have time for.

I don't think that it's fair to them because life gets bad sometimes and I should have warned them when I had the chance. They can't talk yet but I know that they understand me.

The last time I saw them I ended up leaving and fuck, I don't want to be the one responsible for giving them that kind of paranoia every time someone new walks in.

I want to feel better but I've stopped getting ready for bed at seven and falling asleep by nine.

I can't refuse an offer to stay out past ten because I

can't stand the thought of my friends making memories without me, and maybe that's selfish, but sometimes being selfless starts to hurt you while it's helping those around you and I'm so tired of hurting.

I've come to learn that photographs only mean something to the people in them, and that no one bothers to ask who was behind the camera because no one really cares enough to know how one little insecurity can impact a person's perspective so much that they feel obligated to hide behind another's confidence because they cannot find their own.

My mom's talking to a man that I've never met before and the front door stays unlocked at night, but I find it impossible to let myself leave because the ghosts aren't attached to the house, they're attached to me, and they don't live in the walls, they live in my head.

I've started smoking again because I'm sad and tired and hopelessly in love with people that are helplessly in love with themselves.

My skin is momentarily made of sunshine but my heart is an eternal rainstorm and I just want it to stop because inconsistency is frustrating.

And I'm sorry that you'd rather talk to me when I'm doing okay.

I'm sorry that it's hard for me to be okay.

I'd stay okay forever if I could.

We didn't start out as friends, and maybe that's why everything turned to dust.

You called yourself a beast, said that you were incapable of telling me what the fuck was going on in your head, said that despite the uncertainty constantly overshadowing your thoughts you were so fucking certain about me, certain about us.

You told me that I looked beautiful the day I wore a dress, said that you always tried to look good for me and that I should do the same, but I wore sweatpants the next day and you didn't make eye contact with me once.

I let you touch me, let you kiss me in places that I've never been nice to. You said that the marks didn't define me, said that they're a reminder of what I've overcome and you kissed every scar on my body and made me feel whole again. But it was bullshit, because the cracks in my thighs are still there and you didn't heal me at all, only broke me a little more.

You watched my eyes in the rear-view mirror last night because I wouldn't talk to you. I had to force myself to ignore you and not give you the satisfaction of knowing that you won, of you knowing that this was a game I never wanted to play and that you won by using methods such as lying, manipulation, and trust. Methods that have ruined me in the past.

I couldn't hurt like that anymore. I shouldn't have to hurt like that anymore.

I kissed you when everyone told me that you deserved to be hit. I should've swallowed my words instead of spitting them out because second chances aren't given, they're earned, and you did nothing but touch my thigh and tell me that I looked pretty and I fucking lost it. I gave in to you again.

You called yourself a beast the minute you sat down next to me in that hallway, but I disagreed. I empathized with you, let you get close to me like nothing ever went wrong. I told you things that you didn't deserve to hear, because a destroyer does not need healing, the destroyed does.

And you hurt me, taught me that hickies aren't love bites but just bruises. Taught me that fairytales don't always have happy endings. I forgave you, said I didn't hate you, said we could make this work.

But you were a fucking beast, I finally believed you, and I was only ever beautiful when your hands undressed me.

Hear me.

Because I hear your fucking bedroom door slam every goddamn time we disagree on something and the whole fucking house shakes.

I didn't know you were that strong.

Sometimes I wish you would use that strength to lift me up instead of pushing me down.

See me.

Because I see a pack of cigarettes sitting on the porch next to a ceramic bowl I made in seventh grade and you keep flicking your ashes into it like it doesn't even matter.

I created it, and that should be enough to know that embers do not belong in something your kid made for you.

Touch me.

Because I touched a part of you both when I was born but I haven't seen dad in months.

You told me that even though I wasn't planned I was still made from love but we both know that that's bullshit, because if I was made from love then why the fuck am I so angry all the time?

He ignored you when you sent him pictures of me at my first prom and I said that it didn't hurt, but I lied.

I've been good at lying ever since I had to pretend that I didn't see him almost hit you when I was fucking five years old.

Smell me.

Because I smell a mixture of vodka and dirty laundry and it's fucking blocking the whole god damn hallway.

I can't even make it to my bedroom anymore without wanting to vomit first.

You used to love coming home to a clean house but I avoid coming inside and you never even leave your room anymore.

Taste me.

Because the taste of spoiled milk and expired love has taken shelter under my tongue and I want to know that I'm not the only one resisting to swallow.

My stomach is a sea of razors and it's hard to keep food down sometimes.

My family thinks that I'm starving myself again.

Hear me speak.

See me exist.

Touch me where I ask.

Smell my passion.

And taste the stars on my skin.

Because I am not one of the five senses,

I'm all of them.

All of them.

All at once.

he didn't ask if he could kiss me, he just did.

and at that moment i knew that i was being forced
to grow up.

it was like losing my virginity -

only less.

like giving someone a hug -

only more.

he used tongue and no words, only spit.

he was forceful and i almost fell off the concrete
ledge that i was sitting on, but i knew that he
wouldn't have caught me anyway.

he didn't ask if it was okay to touch me, he just did.

my body reacted by breaking out into goosebumps
and he took that as a sign that i liked it, that i
wanted to feel cold, that i was in love with the ice
on his fingertips.

i was too hesitant to speak up, too afraid to stop it...

because how do you say no when a question was
never asked?

he never talked to me about anything important,
never tried to break down any barriers.

he only judged me, let me think that something was
wrong with me, told me to stop being so stubborn
all the damn time.

he never talked to me about anything that went on
internally, only criticized me externally.

and he never asked if he could kiss me, he just did.

the next morning my lips were swollen, but he just
smiled when he walked by.

i'm going to get sad sometimes

and you're going to turn the other way because you

won't know how to handle it

and i'll tell you that it's okay

that your decision to leave doesn't hurt me at all

and maybe at that moment i'll mean it

but it'll hit me so fucking hard tomorrow

and you'll come back to me

but only when i'm not sad anymore

and i'll open my arms and hold you so tight that it'll

feel like you never even left

and you'll kiss me

and i'll let you

but there's only so many hours in a day and

eventually you'll have to go home

and i'll let my arms let you go

even when my mouth is screaming out no because i

can't bear your absence when there's no return date

but you don't seem to hear me

you never do

and you'll call me later that night and we'll talk

about everything

and you'll ask me how i'm feeling and i'll tell you

the truth because you hate it when i lie to you and

so i hesitate

but you encourage me to continue even though i

swear you know that i'm not happy

and so i'll say that i'm sad

and you'll say something along the lines of

"i'm heading to bed goodnight"

and i'll sigh loud enough for you to hear me but

you've hung up by then

and i'll go to sleep hating myself but wake up still

loving you

and you'll be at my door around eleven with coffee

and roses because you know me

you know what i like

and you know that by morning i'm better at hiding

my emotions

and that's when you seem to love me best

i guess i'm just lonely because two days ago he sat across from me in that stupid rocking chair that he claimed as his own and we kissed for the first time in three months.

the porch was dark but i saw a fire behind his eyes and he saw the stars behind mine and the universe was not quiet, it was just paused.

i remember that we were both tired, i from lack of sleep and him from staying sober for more than a week.

i told him how proud of him i was for being surrounded by a trigger but not giving into it, for smelling like his older brother but not standing beside him while he rolled joints in the midst of his friends opening enough beer bottles for a fucking party when there were only four of them in that motel room.

i think i just miss him sometimes even though i feel as if i'm not allowed to because he is not mine and i am not his.

we're both constantly torn between being friends and being partners because he can't keep his hands

to himself when he's around me and i can't stop
spitting out compliments that extend far beyond just
physical.

his smile is not equivalent to his heart but both are
just as crooked, and both are just as capable of
making me feel something strong enough for my
doubts to remain silent.

my best friend keeps telling me that this is just an
addiction, that girls don't fall in love with boys
when we're smart enough to know that they'll be
gone by morning.

and there's never a goodbye kiss, never even a
warning, just an open door that we're too weak to
close in case he decides to come back.

my mind keeps telling me that i'm obsessed with
feeling less alone but my heart swears that i love
him sometimes even if my absence doesn't make
him feel anything at all.

i never know when i'll see him smile again and he
doesn't know how long it'll be until he can hold me
again and neither of us seem to care about that
during the day.

but right now it's midnight and i care too much because he's not sitting across from me in that damn rocking chair and he's not kissing me like he used to.

and we're never really sure if what feels like our first time together could end up being our last because i tend to distance myself and he doesn't like to answer his phone.

but we try not to think about that when the sun's up, we don't want to.

Maybe it was never meant to work out, right?

I mean, we hopped over our friend's fence to smoke cigarettes behind bushes last night and you called me ugly. I just laughed and said "I know." But later that night you said "You're cute, you know that?" And I just said "Thank you," because usually I'm the one giving mixed signals instead of receiving them, and you knew it, too.

Four days ago we dived head first into an empty pool and I think that we're both still suffering from the effects of it, because you bring up invalid points and I accuse you of things that aren't entirely true. You said it yourself, I'm not ready for a relationship, so why do you keep begging me to come back? I put the caution sign up when I let you kiss me for the first time, but you forced your way through my front door and it's not my fault that you ended up slipping.

My phone used to blow up with "I miss you" texts and pointless fucking voicemails until he cut me off when I refused to have sex with him, even after he begged me to. He thought that I would find the image of him on his knees endearing, as if his persistence on getting inside of my pants would make me wet without him even having to touch me, but the thought of his hands coming anywhere near me turned me off completely, and I made damn sure that he knew it, too.

Maybe it was never meant to work out, right?

I mean, boys will chase you down and step on your toes and then apologize when they hurt you, but they'll never stay around long enough to clean up the mess, and you'll bleed because of it and they'll come back, but only once the blood has dried and the wounds have healed.

And maybe that's why it was never meant to work out, you know?

Because I don't need a boy to kiss any part of my body in hopes to make it better and then complain about the shards of glass on his lips. I don't want a boy to think that I need him, because I don't.

Women don't need men. Women don't need men.

And I don't need those careless boys to try and please me when I know how to please myself better than any of them can.

Their dirty fingers just roam...

my pretty little fingers dance.

Sometimes I look at myself and all I can think about is how disgusting my body is,

and so I won't eat for a few hours but then I'll think "this isn't healthy,"

and my stomach will growl,

and I'll feel bad for neglecting its needs,

and so I'll eat,

and I'll feel proud of myself,

but then I'll see a picture of a girl online and I'll become sad, jealous...

Or I'll be out with friends and see a girl's thighs before I see her face and I'll feel bad for putting my desires over her personality,

but I won't apologize because by then I'm already looking at some other girl's stomach and I'll envy her because I'd rather die than expose a part of me that I hate to the public.

And so I won't eat for a day,

but then I'll feel guilty for treating my body like that,

and it's an endless cycle.

I know that we all hate some part of ourselves,

and I know that it's okay.

That it's normal.

But we shouldn't spend our time envying a body
when we have our own,

instead we should envy the way someone displays
confidence or the way that someone dedicates their
time to bettering themselves,

and then we should turn that envy into inspiration,

motivation.

We should learn from them and better ourselves,
too.

You're beautiful.

I swear to you that you're beautiful.

Your body is eternal, okay?

Stop treating it like it's temporary.

i need you to understand that

none of this is your fault

that what you said about me

is absolutely true

and that the realization of it

finally fucking hit me

because how could i allow myself to become

so toxic and so vile

that my own best friend

had to call me apathetic

in order to help me realize

that i am not good

i have never been good

and i will never be good

i walk around thinking that people are

greater than i am

that i have somehow managed to

make myself insignificant

but that's false

because i'm still leaving footprints in the cement

and i'm still getting phone calls

from family members that i've never even met

i've somehow convinced myself

that i'm not the thunderstorm

but rather the calm before it

the gentle breeze before the power goes out

the quiet knocking of trees against a window

but that's false too

because i am both the before and the after

i need you to understand that

i never meant to hurt you

but by doing so

i've come to hate myself in a way

that i never thought possible

in a way that is unfathomable

in a way that is beyond anything i could ever put

into words

unless i find a profound enough sentence to describe

what it is i see when i look into the mirror

a monster

a tragedy

a reclusive individual

that thrives off of pleasure and broken promises

you have to understand

that i don't always understand why i'm like this

why i'm so fucking stubborn

why i'm so goddamn explosive

and maybe it's easier

to blame it on the past

or the drugs

or the alcohol

and perhaps someday

i'll be able to take full responsibility

for what i've done

because this is all my fault

and i know that it's my fault

and i'm not trying to play the victim

because i know that

i don't fulfill that role anymore

and i know that i'm not the hero either

so can you please tell me

what that makes me

can you tell me

where that leaves you

My first kiss with A was next to a trash can while he balanced his bike with one foot on the ground.
He pushed my hair out of my eyes and said

"Are you going to kiss me?"

And so I leaned in.

A quick peck and an unsteady heartbeat was normal for a 13-year-old, I thought.

My first kiss with C was on a brick ledge in front of someone's house.

He had a cigarette in one hand and his phone in the other.

"I'll give you a real kiss,"

he said with too much enthusiasm, and so he did.

He sucked me in as if a real kiss meant all tongue, no passion.

All spit, no love.

I didn't enjoy it much at the age of 15.

My first kiss with R was in a secluded area outside while everyone else continued drinking inside.

I wanted to ignore him, resist him, but I couldn't and he encouraged me with the words

"Don't worry, she won't find out."

The taste of alcohol on his tongue and the smell of weed on his clothes made me trust him, but she found out about the affair two months after my 17th birthday.

He had told her about it.

My first kiss with J was on my best friend's sister's bed during a game of truth or dare.

I told him that I never skip a challenge and he nodded in agreement, said he liked my bravery.

I picked dare and he replied with

"Don't be such a pussy, come on, they're not looking."

And so he made out with me while our friends watched us from behind the closet door.

I felt uncomfortable doing this at the age of 16.

My first kiss with N was on my couch in the living

room while a movie played in the background.

He had other intentions and whispered

"This'll be fun, trust me"

into my ear.

I trusted him, and it was fun at the age of 17, but he hasn't talked to me since.

My first kiss with D was in the front seat of his car at midnight while he was high.

We didn't talk much…

we didn't have to, and he pulled me in and kissed me until I was dizzy and forgot about every bad moment I ever had trying to do this the right way.

The raw sensation of lips on lips and the feeling of lust and the thoughts that scream:

"I like this moment."

"I want this moment forever."

"I want to see them again."

"I want to see them always…"

I had felt that at 18.

It was beautiful, dangerous.

But he dates my best friend now and they're off making out somewhere in a parking lot.

But I'm okay.

I'm almost 19 and I've learned that I should wait for a boy who asks if it's okay to kiss me before leaning in.

i'm writing this to inform you that i am happy

beyond happy

my happiness is opaque

only few can see it

some can even feel it

it's brilliantly morbid

undoubtedly addictive

it's beautiful

i am so happy

i no longer find mason jars full of tears in my closet

and my hangers are just hangers now

they don't hold the various masks that i used to

strategically place

waiting for the right hour to be sewn upon my face

now they just hold clothes

bright clothes

clothes pretty enough to attract wanted

and overdue attention

but never loud enough to hold a stranger's gaze for

more than ten seconds

a flick of the head and a wisp of hair in the breeze

for they see me

yet they do not know me (dare i ever let them)

i'm writing this to inform you that i am happy

disgustingly happy

it's contagious

hauntingly pleasant

i no longer wish to fly from atop a building in fear

that i may hurt another in the process of trying to

hurt myself

i could never let myself end such a magical life with

such a tragic beginning

you must know that i do not want a funeral

when i die

for i wish not to stain the lives of my loved ones

who are so clean

i used to be so miserable

it was harsh

uninviting

cold

i wanted to be warm

comfortably warm

i wanted to become welcoming

so welcoming i became

i welcomed happiness as if it were a guest in my

home

it spread throughout my body with every inhale and

never left me when i exhaled

i welcomed happiness when i started opening

prescription pill bottles instead of opening kitchen

drawers in search of the sharpest knife

i welcomed happiness when i began to feel free

with every step away from home i took

i never looked back

i felt alive

alive

such a foreign feeling

but absolutely lovely nonetheless

i'm writing this to inform you that i am happy

so happy

daringly and sickeningly happy

i trust you to not take this happiness away from me

please do not take this away from me

it took years to build up

it'd be a pity if you knocked it all down

don't ask me to stay

because i won't

i don't know how to

don't tell me you miss me

because i'll lie and say that i miss you too

but the truth is

i don't know how to

don't call me when you're sad

because i won't comfort you

i don't know how to

don't start apologizing in hopes that i'll forgive you

because i won't

i don't know how to

don't tell your friends that i'm a terrible person

that i'm a fuck up

that you're better off without me

because i won't defend myself

i don't know how to

and don't come back a month from now telling me

that you still love me

that you want to try again

because it won't change my mind about you

because i won't love you back

i don't know how to

Be pretty, be soft, they said.

Don't spit on the sidewalk, just swallow it.

Swallow it like you would your pride.

Don't sit like that, they told me.

Men will think you're easy, they'll want you and
they won't stop until they have you.

By force or by permission, it does not matter.

Sitting with your legs open instead of crossed only
gives them permission to fantasize, to take
advantage of the view.

Sit proper, they said.

Sit like a lady, they warned.

Sit like you've never been touched before, like
you're still pure.

Don't talk about sex, they said.

Stop being so open minded and blunt, just keep
your damn mouth shut.

But I didn't listen, I kept talking.

Saying anything they deemed as inappropriate just to get a rise out of them, just to prove that they do not control what comes out of my mouth.

Girls aren't supposed to talk about what happens in the bedroom, they kept saying.

But I let the dirtiest words that I know spill from my pretty, pink lips.

The same lips that were performing un lady-like acts on a man the other night.

Don't eat all of that.

Even a guy couldn't finish that much food, they kept saying.

Stop hanging around boys so much.

They'll either think you're a slut or that you're trying too hard to be one of them, they kept reminding me.

Believe them when they call you names, okay?

Let it change you.

Let it get to you.

Let it hurt you, they said, pounding the words into my skull until the idea of who I was supposed to be and who I wanted to be started blending into one.

Be pretty, be soft, they had the nerve to say.

But they never told me that I could be rough and cruel when I needed to be, that it was okay to be the reason for someone else's tears instead of being the one always shedding them.

They never reminded me that it was okay to be strong, that I didn't always have to play the role of someone I knew I'd never become.

And that's the most damaging thing that you could do to a girl, you know?

Tell them who to be before they even have the chance to figure it out on their own, tear apart their dignity before they even have time to build it up.

i thought i loved him

when he said

"fuck, you're so beautiful, round 2?"

so i let him touch me

because i didn't know how not to

i thought i loved him

when he made me breathless

and my stomach hurt too much to laugh it off

his fists felt rougher than before

but his eyes were still just as soft

i thought i loved him

when he came home late

because it gave me something to look forward to

but he never looked directly at me

when he walked in

just grabbed a beer and went into the bedroom

i thought i loved him

when he rubbed his fingers over my knuckles

ignoring the shades of purple and blue

he never asked where the bruises came from

because he didn't want to hear me lie

when we both knew the truth

i thought i loved him

when my friends said

"you can't fix him"

because i remembered that time i made him smile

it was a year ago

maybe two

but he hasn't done it in a while

i thought i loved him

when i heard him crying in the shower

even though he never cried in front of me

i knew that he was afraid of coming off as weak

but sometimes

at least once

i needed him to be

and i thought i loved him

when he told me that he cared

although it never showed

i convinced myself that he's just a little broken

the best broken piece i own

and i realized i didn't love him

when he smelled of perfume

and yelled at me as if i were a kid

i realized i didn't love him

when someone told me to go home

and i finally fucking did

i'm better

things don't hurt as much as they used to

instead of walking on glass i'm now sipping from it

the blood on my thighs are wine and i no longer cry
but rather give a toast to the marvelous shades of
red

i'm doing well

my friends don't worry about me like they used to,
instead they envy me, for they long to be as happy
as i am

i'm so happy

i don't need my pills anymore; i'm so much better
off without them

no more blue, no more red, no more yellow

no more throwing up in fear that if they stay down,
i'll feel down

i hide them under my tongue and spit them out as
soon as my mother closes her bedroom door

she seems to ignore the fact that i take out my trash
quite often

she doesn't seem to notice that the bag is never
actually full

i'm better

the bad things i do no longer terrify me but rather
excite me

they keep me awake when it's midnight and
someone asks me how my day went

my stories belong in books with coffee stained
pages and ink scribbles in the margins

no

they belong in something much larger, in a place
where everyone can read them

i'm okay, really i am

i don't get sad anymore...i don't cry either

i just laugh so loud that people question it even
though i never have an appropriate response

i'm okay

i'm beautifully young and indefinitely infinite

i'm in tune with my surroundings

i'm everywhere and i'm in everything

my body is strong and my mind is powerful

i'm better. i'm so much better

I don't want to write sad poetry anymore because I'm happy, but I can't stop crying at night.

I guess I'm just tired of wiping away everyone's tears while mine fall.

I guess I'm tired of pretending that listening to my friends vent about the same shit every day doesn't stress me out at all.

He told me he was sorry and I said that it was okay, that he's my friend and if he needed to get over his ex I was happy to help.

I'm just glad that he touched me instead of touching a girl that would have fallen for him in that moment of lust and lies.

I don't care that he used me, and I guess that says more about me than it does about him.

This boy from Pennsylvania said he kinda liked me and when I reminded him that he doesn't do well with feelings he just said

"I don't know."

It shouldn't bother me that he's fucking some other

girl while I'm lying in bed, because I tried to prepare myself for it, I tried not to like him back, but sometimes your heart is not capable of shutting down even when you beg it to.

I've learned that distance doesn't bring two people together, it just tears them apart.

Phone calls and text messages aren't good enough if you can't even hear the way their heart beats for you.

My mom painted her walls pink and my initial reaction was bitterness.

The once tan walls are now glowing and the darkened shades are always open.

She wanted to make it look more like a nursery for my baby sister, but the color makes me sick.

I can't stand it when she leaves her door open.

My old friends don't remember me, but all I seem to do is remember the way they once gave a shit about me.

They're in new groups and they seem so much

happier. I'm happy for them, so why the fuck does it sting so bad?

I don't want to write sad poetry.

I shouldn't be writing sad poetry, but I don't feel in control.

I don't have the kind of emotions I once did and instead of breaking down completely, I just cry gently.

I don't shake unless his hands are running down my body and I don't use words anymore, but rather let my tongue do the talking.

I don't want to write sad poetry again but my head hurts.

I've gone numb.

I don't think about razor blades and pills anymore but I don't think about sunshine and flowers, either.

I barely even have time to think about myself.

I don't feel guilty when people tell me that I've gone heartless, you know?

Or when they remind me that I've changed.

I am who I am because of what I've done, and I'm learning how to cope with the pain.

i'm watching my mom collapse under the weight

of her pregnancy

she fell asleep in the tub

two days ago

but denies it even though

i heard her snoring

through the walls

i told her not to take baths when i'm out with friends

but tonight i came home

to running water

and a flooded bathroom floor -

hours later and she still denies dreaming

i'm watching an old friend

get back together

with a man that didn't

break her heart

but rather tore it

just enough to keep her

from going insane

i listened to her

talk about love like it was some kind of drug

that she was already

addicted to

i listened to her stories of innocent kisses turning

into two-hour arguments

and promised myself that i'd never get hooked on

something so dangerous

something that

life threatening

i'm watching the days

pass by me like

a stop motion video

some parts aren't

lined up right and

others are just missing

i try to fill in the gaps with adventures and

rebellious nights

but when i look back

all i see are the plans that fell through lying

somewhere beneath the pile of

clothes on my bed

i'm watching him

struggle with getting over her

he comes to me for advice and leaves me alone

when he's got it

i listen to him talk about how manipulative she is

but remind him that he still answers the phone

whenever she calls

he picks it up on the first ring

knowing that she'll start the

conversation with a cry

rather than a word

and then he'll come to me wondering why the fuck

he's hurting so bad

even though i've told him

time and time again

that he can't move on

if he keeps letting her

back in

he says she's a devil but seems to forget

that they always sin

i'm watching my life

through eyes that have not slept in two days

through eyes that have cried for three weeks straight

through eyes that just want

to hold someone's gaze instead of feeling forced

to look away

through eyes that cannot speak but have so much

to say

and i'm watching myself

fade in and out of consciousness

it's like i'm here when people need something

but i no longer exist when they're okay

it's like i'm always there for

everyone else

but when i need help

they've all gone away

I'm sitting in class when a boy comes up to me
asking if I'd ever have a one-night stand with him.

I'm taken aback because I was just sitting here
writing down notes and I don't know what led him
to cross the room in order to ask me a question that
makes me doubt my self worth.

Does all he see is my body, my dress?

What about the way my eyes light up when I laugh?

What about my heart?

I breathe in, out, look him in the eyes and say

"Not with you."

But he doesn't flinch, just says,

"What if it's three nights?"

As if I'd willingly spend two seconds alone with
him, as if I'm flattered that he abandoned his class
work to make me feel a little less human.

Where is the decency?

Where is the respect?

I'm walking down the hallway when a boy I used to
be friends with in seventh grade says,

"Damn."

in regard to my outfit.

I smile because I'm uncomfortable.

I don't look behind me even though I can feel his eyes traveling down my backside.

I know how he is with women... reckless, emotionless.

He never says anything to me when I come to school in sweatpants and it makes me wonder if a tight dress is all it takes for a boy to acknowledge me.

To want me.

I'm waiting for my ride when a boy from my tech class says,

"Go home."

It's a mixture of stern and flirty, something I've taught myself to avoid.

I flip him off because I don't want to speak to him, I don't want to look at him, and he responds with

"When?"

as if he doesn't have a girlfriend that's loyal enough
to be late to class every day just to kiss him a little
longer.

I say,

"You're not funny."

and he laughs because he thinks that sexual jokes
are humorous even when I'm visibly uneasy.

All I want to do is make it home without feeling a
little less human.

I want to burn my fucking dress.

Why do boys have to say things like

"Who are you trying to impress?"

and

"Why'd you get all dressed up?"

Why can't they just say

"You look nice today."

and leave it at that?

I'm dressed like this for me, never for you.

Why treat us like objects?

Why make us feel scared to leave our house in a dress?

Why make us feel less human than you?

Why not just treat us with respect?

she is both

the insomniac

and the

dreamer

the wide awake

sleeper

the breath following

a saddened stare

for you know

you cannot

keep her

she's the

tilted chin

at midnight

fingers touching skin

wind slamming

a concrete door

for she'll

never let you in

she's a sign

without a label

intriguing

yet unable

to fall for anything

close to sturdy

for she's always

been unstable

she's the scent

of cigarette smoke

burning holes

through your

wooden frame

she wakes up

in your bed again

but whispers

another's name

she's a hurricane

of power

setting fire

to the hearts

of men

tattooing her face

on every surrounding

so they'll never

crave anyone

except for her

again

and again

and again

you deserve to know that you're beautiful

that your touch burns me up

from icy cold fingertips

to a body made of heat

you do that to me

only you

your smile is

intoxicating

addicting

warm

i photograph you when you're laughing

it reminds me that even on my worst days

i can always count on that smile to get me through

whatever's weighing me down

just a simple curve of your lips

can save me from drowning

i hope you know that

sometimes i hate you for doing this to me

for making me want to hold your hand

in front of my family and kiss you

in front of strangers

sometimes i hate you for making me

want to do nice things for you

like make you playlists and

leave love notes on your whiteboard

but i don't hate you

not at all

you just make me feel so much

that i think i might be sick

but you're always there

to hold my hair back

when i find it hard to keep everything in

i don't like it when people look at you

because they can't see how radiant you truly are

i don't think that i'll ever get used to the way the

sun hides in shame when it's near you

for you're the brightest

you must know that

you make me so weak

i want to lie down in the middle of the street with

you and talk about everything

but i don't

you make me feel strong enough to resist putting

myself in danger

how do you do that

make me feel like

the damned

and the saved

all at once

your sheets smell like safety

your arms feel like home

we laugh for what seems like hours

because it usually is

you don't want to leave and i have a hard time

unlocking the car door

but neither of us mind

"text me when you get home"

goodbyes and

"i'm proud of you" hugs and

"i miss you" phone calls

we're so close

no matter the growing distance

we've always got time for each other

i'll always make time for you

you've gotta know that

we let our eyes find the perfection

hidden beneath the other's skin

let our actions explain what our words cannot

it's beautiful and innocent

familiar and comforting

you deserve to know that you're the best thing that's

ever came into my life

okay?

and i'd really like it if you stayed

I want to talk about you and all the ways you make me feel.

I want to kiss you until you're dizzy and you taste how much I appreciate everything you say to me, even if it hurts.

Know that I'd listen for a lifetime if it meant I got to feel your lips on mine in between sentences.

I want to thank you for putting your life on hold there to call me here, to listen to me cry and comfort me at the same time.

Your voice is more than a whisper down the line, it's an echo that lays next to me when I find it hard to sleep, when you're already asleep, when I miss you and my bed feels like it's drifting through space because yours feels like home.

Familiarity.

You smell like happiness and your skin feels like cotton beneath my fingertips.

You talk to me from behind the shower curtain and aggressively sing the wrong lyrics to the easiest songs.

Thank you for checking the backseat of my car when it's late and I'm a little too paranoid to drive home on my own.

I like it when you're near me, when you kiss my forehead and my cheek and say "one more," even though we both know it's never the last one.

That time you hugged me in the middle of a crowded gym because I looked like I needed a hug. I'm glad you see me when I'm sweaty and insecure, but somehow still beautiful in your eyes.

Thank you for motivating me, for letting me be sad but also being persistent enough to help me realize that I am so much more than who hurt me.

I'm okay, I'm better now.

I tell you that I photograph pretty things and you are the most beautiful thing that I've ever had the pleasure of capturing.

It's okay if you go away someday, a photo of you laughing is enough to make the bad days feel a little less bad.

Thank you for trusting me, for letting me scan my thumb print into your phone, for letting me use your laptop for a school project, for leaving the door to your heart unlocked whenever I'm around.

Thank you for being weird and for resting your head on my lap when we're sitting on a park bench.

Thank you for touching me carefully and for offering to paint my nails.

Thank you for letting me constantly talk about you because I'm obsessed with what you do to me.

Thank you for not only letting me fall, but for falling with me.

Sometimes all it takes is the flutter of a butterfly's wings against your wrist to feel whole again.

You keep the porch light on when I come home late, like a lighthouse, as if I'm lost at sea. Like a message, saying, "Come home baby, come home to me." So I do, because you love me and I love you, and the distance between the front door to my bedroom is too long for me to walk alone, so you leave me with a glow, to guide me through the old photographs of my father and the tears that have stained the living room carpet.

It's been building up for years, that barrier between you and me. And you lay in bed, still as can be, mind quiet, heart a little lost, listening to the floorboards creak under the weight of your little girl who is no longer a little girl - and I do not feel whole.

The butterfly's wings feel like razor blades against my skin.

Sometimes all it takes is the faintest scent of a person you love to make you smile.

A mixture of safety and comfort traveling through the wind, making you want to bottle up the smell and save it for a lonely night when it's storming out and you find yourself unable to dream of pretty things.

I look at guys when I'm out with friends, but then I remember that they're not you, and I get angry, because they're closer to me than you are and all I want to do is hold your hand.

This longing, this ache to kiss you on every busy street corner, to admire you when it's dark out and a car drives by, illuminating your eyes and the way they're looking into mine, to openly admit that I feel so deeply for you I must've gotten stuck at the bottom - does not make me smile. Your presence makes me smile, it is your absence that sews my lips shut.

Wearing your shirt to bed is not enough. The smell fades, and the fabric is suffocating, and I want your skin against mine, freeing me from the sadness I feel when we say goodnight and I'm forced to drive the image of you away.

Make me feel whole again.

Sometimes moments are not enough. And memories are not enough. And people and dandelions and shooting stars are not enough. Some days nothing is enough, but sometimes, if you're really lucky, and things fall into place, nothing becomes something, and that will always be enough.

it's like driving with your eyes closed

not a blink

just falling asleep behind the wheel

it's like speeding at 5 am

or 5 pm

both are just as fatal

like fixing your rear view mirror at a stop sign

like putting all your weight on the brakes

instead of on the gas

because sometimes waiting

is safer than continuation

it's like putting on your high beams

when it's a saturday morning

like making a wrong turn down a one way

like every song on the radio melted away and

left you nothing but static

constant blackness screaming at you

through your speakers

like a flat tire without a spare in the trunk

like being pulled over a block away

from your house while your friends are in the car

like finally hitting 95 on a highway

before the brakes fail

before the windows shatter

before all you taste is metal between your teeth

before it hits you that the crash was anticipated

but never prepared for

it's like driving with your eyes closed

you and me

like shutting off the car only to hear his name echo

in the passenger seat

like sitting at a yellow light for seven hours

like being late to your own party

because you got stuck in traffic

like unbuckling then re buckling your seatbelt

every time uncertainty hits

like never being quite sure if you should

take the risk while knowing the consequences

or if you should play it safe

while feeling like the loneliest person in the world

i took the risk

and i'm still feeling the effects of

my decision in my sleep

still seeing the damage i could have prevented

in my dreams

A year ago we were at a party and you followed me into the bathroom. You said,"I miss you," so I kissed you, but three weeks later your number was blocked.

Eleven months ago I had to watch my mom struggle with finding a job. I held back on going out because even after working a double shift for two months, we were still too short on money to fix the heater that broke down in the middle of December.

Ten months ago I refused to curse because my grandmother had told me that it was impolite, but sometimes when you hang around people who only provide darkness for so long, you'll begin to notice that your light will dim, too.

Nine months ago I got high on a bridge with some friends and my mom didn't seem to notice that I came home an hour after my curfew. She was passed out in her bed with the guy whose truck was parked out front.

Eight months ago I met a man on the boardwalk that tried feeling me up before he even asked for my name. His buddies said that he hasn't gotten laid in months and I walked away with the words "Fuck, I wonder why… " trailing behind me.

Seven months ago my ex and I decided on being friends with benefits, but two weeks later he was dating my best friend. I haven't kissed anyone since then and I can't stand the fact that his fingerprints are still all over my body.

Six months ago I tried reconnecting with an old friend, but she just kept sending me to voicemail. I couldn't remember what I did to make her hate me so much but she wasn't the first one to give me a permanent silent treatment. I had gotten used to it real fast.

Five months ago I relapsed in the shower and my mom believed me when I said that the razor had slipped. I've learned how to make something intentional look accidental even though my knee caps were far too scarred for the occasional 'blade mishap.'

Four months ago my dad stopped calling and I stopped caring. I don't miss him like I used to but I miss my siblings, and I don't need my father but my siblings need me. I don't know where they are or if they're safe or if they even remember who I am. It's a fucking avalanche of pain, a constant stream of guilt for leaving them even though it was never my fault that I had to go.

Three months ago I started punching things instead of crying and my friend's bathroom walls still have dents in them because she can't afford to get it fixed, but she didn't kick me out like everyone else had, she just held me and reminded me that everything was going to be okay, even though she knew I didn't believe her.

Two months ago I got called apathetic by someone who I once called my best friend. We had sleepovers in his car and talked about our fucked-up lives, but now he's changing his while I'm not changing mine. I'm just waiting for it to end, I think.

One month ago I decided to remove the word love from my vocabulary, but last night I got so drunk that the moment seemed right. I slipped on the idea of something good happening for once, but he kept his balance and walked away. I didn't chase after him and I didn't try calling him, either.

I learned that if you let a person deny you for too long, you'll start to deny yourself, too.

That if you give everything you have to someone you think you love, you'll feel like you have nothing to lose, but there is always something to lose, and once it's gone, you will never get it back.

i stayed up for hours waiting to hear your voice

waiting for you to call me back at 11:15

but it's a school night and i haven't slept in two days
and last night's homework is still sitting on my desk
in the corner of the room

and i am tired

yet i wait for a call that never comes

and the next morning you say you got caught up
with work but you don't apologize and i just smile

and two weeks later i happen to look at your phone
and you're texting the girl that stared at you a bit too
long at that party we went to one night

and your fingers dance around the letters on your
phone screen as if you're fabricating a sentence that
she won't forget reading

as if you care about her opinion of you more than
mine

as if you want her opinion of you to be one of
greatness rather than one of insignificance

and it seems as if you forget that i'm sitting right
next to you on your own couch in your own living
room in your own apartment

and i can't think and i can't breathe and you don't
ask me why my hands are shaking or why we
haven't spoke since you unlocked the door and let
me in

and so i find myself using the excuse of

"i'm going to the bathroom"

when really i'm headed towards the back door

and you don't seem to hear it open nor do you seem
to notice that i'm walking in the opposite direction
of my destination and i can't focus on anything but
the cigarette that i'm smoking on your back porch
and the way your face lit up the minute your phone
screen did

and five minutes later you come out and sit next to
me in one of those ugly green chairs that your mom
bought you as a housewarming gift

and you don't seem to look at me but rather through
me and you take the cigarette that's dangling
between my lips and crush it beneath your boot on
the ground

and you speak for the first time that night saying

"it's cold out here isn't it"

as if i didn't know that you had a habit of asking

rhetorical questions when you were thinking of
something else and wanted to move on from
whatever situation presented itself as uncomfortable

as if you really wanted an obvious response of

"yes it is"

as if the goosebumps on my skin were from the
overwhelming sensation of your presence rather
than from my lack of winter attire

and i am sad because you don't offer me your jacket
but instead wrap it tighter around yourself and tell
me to come inside soon

you retrieve the pack of cigarettes from my lap and
reopen it only to discover that i have three left
despite buying it last week and you light one up for
yourself and walk away leaving me alone to let my
tears turn to ice falling unnoticed and uncared for

and i can't stop shaking and i can't comprehend
what happened between us and i can't breathe

and so i walk home that night despite my
temptations to stay and talk to you because i know
that you're talking to her

and when i get home i stay up for hours anticipating
a phone call from you that i know will never come
and the homework that was assigned weeks ago still

remains untouched on my desk in the corner of the room and i don't care

and the next morning i find out that you didn't get caught up with work but instead spent your evening catching up with her

and you weren't calling me back because you were too busy touching her

and you never got the chance to end it with me because you were more focused on starting something with her

and i can't breathe and i can't breathe and i can't fucking breathe because i'm in love with you

but you're falling in love with her

I don't want to be sad, but sometimes hands don't always stay soft and gentle hearts have hidden thorns.

I promised my friends that I wouldn't drink too much because of what happened last time, but two hours later I'm stumbling around the house shaking hands with every unfamiliar face I come across.

I apologized for letting them down, for going against my word, but apologies don't mean shit if you already fucked up, you know?

I've always been too stubborn not to try. I think I'm just afraid of looking like the bad guy.

I spent more time parading around with a bottle in my hand when I should have been engaging in conversation downstairs.

I wore high waisted jeans because I thought that it would keep me protected. Thought that even the slightest bit of a struggle would disinterest any determined male, but I was wrong.

The house was cold but nobody bothered to close the windows.

Trails of air lingered from everyone's mouth when they talked but no one could hear anything anyway, no one really cared, either.

My fingers wouldn't stop shaking that night, but neither would the rest of my body.

A fight almost broke out in the kitchen an hour after the party started.

Two juniors from my school were spitting out words across the counter, words that I haven't heard since my separated parents decided to 'talk it out' over the phone two weeks ago.

The one guy didn't care if he ended up in jail but death isn't temporary, you know?

I think the alcohol made them both feel immortal.

The guy I liked broke my heart a half an hour after the fight blew over, but I can't really blame him.

He's known for being careless with girls, but I thought that I could change him, and I did, but only when we were in his bed at 2:30 in the morning after a night of drinking.

I passed him on my way to the bathroom and he looked at me like he didn't even know my name, like he's never seen me before, like the evidence of him being under my shirt was a lie that I had fabricated, like he wasn't crying in my arms two weeks ago because he was overwhelmed with how much he felt for me, like he didn't really care that he lost me.

I collapsed on the staircase because everything was so fucking suffocating, you know?

I don't think there's a better way to describe the atmosphere of a house filled with tension.

I cried in front of classmates that I grew up with but never talked to.

Panic attacks are so scary when you don't know whose words are trying to calm you down, when you don't know whose hands are trying to help you up.

I remember pressing my back against the wall in an attempt to make the world stop spinning so fast, but there was no way to stop it.

I felt like a dam that had just broke; I no longer had control over my emotions and that's exactly what happens when you don't let yourself cry for months, it spills. Everything around you caves in and you don't care that you're sitting in the middle of the floor crying while the people around you are getting high in the midst of all the empty beer bottles.

Sometimes the house you enter ends up becoming your grave, but my friends wouldn't let me die that night, even though I wanted to.

I was supposed to be home by 11:30 but my eyes revealed the secrets that my mouth would lie about and I couldn't hurt my mom like that.

I don't know how I ended up in the backseat of my friend's car, but I do know that I woke up safe in my best friend's bed. She held me, you know? Really held me and in that moment I didn't care if my ribs were cracking because she made me feel whole, made me feel okay.

I know that most days things aren't okay, but I also know that I can't move forward if I keep dwelling too much on the past.

I don't want to be sad, you know?

But sometimes when you're surrounded by tempting substances and triggering people you're going to let yourself give in.

I have to stop letting myself give in.

I think at age eleven we were more focused on where we should sit in the cafeteria rather than who was going to skip lunch that day.

My friends would rotate starving themselves, always saying, "I'll eat when I get home." I got tired of questioning them, so I just kept my eyes on the clock instead.

Transitioning from elementary school to middle school proved harder than it seemed.

For some reason I couldn't remember my locker combination but I could remember the design under the kid's boot that sat behind me. Usually friends say, "See you later!" I guess acquaintances would rather leave their mark.

My cousin graduated last year and he's still not in college.

I keep thinking that maybe he's just busy, that he'll get around to it, but I've seen numerous unopened envelopes in the trashcan and I'm starting to think that he's just too hopeless to try. That's sad, I guess.

Being a freshman was like trying to navigate your way through a maze in the dark. We weren't all annoying, some of us just wanted to become greater without coming off as egotistical.

There was a boy in my history class that always looked at me.

My heart usually skipped long enough to miss whatever was written on the board, but the teacher never seemed to notice. The next day he had a girl that didn't like me latched onto his arm and he smiled at her like he smiled at me. But I didn't cry. Sometimes people do things that hurt us, my dad taught me that years ago.

I had a friend whose name sounded a lot like mine.

One day she cried so much that I thought we'd both drown. Her head was in my lap and my jeans acted as a tissue and she sniffled and said that she was sorry. A fifteen-year-old girl shouldn't be crying that much, but she's sketching her life in pen when she should be using a pencil. I tell her that I love her every day. Sometimes there just aren't enough words to heal a wound.

I find myself breaking more bones than objects these days, and most of the time they're not even mine.

He kissed me in the back seat of his car while sirens blared in the background. I became uneasy, but he just kept touching me.

Sometimes I forget that a bed is meant for sleeping in. I spend hours arguing with my sheets when I should be putting my clothes away.

At age seventeen we were more obsessed with fake nails and parties when we should have been figuring out which boy raped the girl.

We'd all heard about it, but no one spoke up, and one day she just left. I still think about her when it rains.

Things don't always work out the way you want them to, you know?

Sometimes you're not strong enough to hold yourself up, but neither are the people around you, I guess.

the world slows down at night

leaving your mind to fill the absence of

conversation and expression

darkness enters and you want to welcome it

let it cover you like a blanket

but you feel the wrongness of it all

you feel the familiarity of coldness and realize that

you are not the one exposing your skin to the

atmosphere of the room

something is tugging at your clothes

grasping at your ankles

weighing you down in ways

that cause you to drown without ever being given

the opportunity to float

your closet door becomes a visitation room

kept hidden behind a rusty lock

to meet with them means to meet with uncertainty

and you're too numb to move

too paralyzed to feel

too scared that if you enter

they won't let you leave

the voices you hear aren't distant noises

traveling with the wind

but rather your thoughts trying to find

comfortability in empty spaces

that have yet to be claimed

they are a gentle reminder

that you are not alone

that you are not alone

not alone

not alone

not alone no matter how hard

you slam your bedroom door behind you

after using the bathroom

without turning on the light

for in fear that if you do

you'll catch sight of something else in

the reflection of the mirror

something uglier than your perception of yourself

not alone no matter how tightly you shut the blinds

before settling into bed

for in fear that if you don't

someone will be bold enough

to climb up to your window

in search of tainted innocence

and vivid imaginations

and broken fantasies

caught in the web of a hanging dream catcher

not alone no matter how convinced

you are that you are safe

that no one can see your chest rising and falling

a little too quickly in the dark

that no one can hear your

heart pounding against every inch

of your skin violently

like a wild animal

kept sheltered in a cage for so long

that everyone around him

has forgotten about his existence

not alone

never alone at night

you are surrounded by eyes that cannot understand

what they are seeing

but rather feeling your emotions through

the vibrations that you unknowingly give off

this is how they decipher what to do next

hurt you or heal you

harm you or help you

and then it's six am

and your room is soaked with sunlight

and the smell of saturday morning breakfast

and you can breathe again

but no one is talking

and no one is tugging at your ankles

and your closet door is just another place for storage

and your bedroom is still and

everything is still

everything is still

and the world slows down at night

this we have come to know

so why when daytime finally hits

do we feel the most alone

I was taught to be obedient at a young age. Say "please" and "thank you." Listen when I'm being spoken to. Stay quiet when I wanted to say something - but I taught myself that one.

This belief led to fears, phobias that I still struggle with today.

I used to be afraid of individualism, because conforming to my environment seemed easier than being myself.

But who was I? Who am I?

I used to be counseling. Hours spent lying to a lady that knew my name but not my dreams. A lady who ate my mother's money while I left feeling robbed of more than just cash.

I used to be sleep deprived, nervous that while I was unconscious, I'd miss everything. Someone would die. Life would shatter and I wouldn't be aware of it happening. I wouldn't be able to stop it. Paranoia, they call it. I wear it on my face. I get it from my grandmother. We both find our hands shaking a lot and our heartbeats out of control. We're never calm, we don't know how to relax.

I have this theory that there is a correlation between development and displacement.

I grow, but I do not fit in. I stand, but I must shift. I have to move away. I need to leave this town.

I don't want to find expired medications on the bathroom counter anymore or feel whatever positive self-esteem I have left drain out of me every time I pass a reflective surface - it's pure frustration.

My memory is flooded with behaviors I wish weren't tied to my name. I want to cut the string, let these past conflicts unravel in the wind. Let myself feel free, weightless.

I was taught to sit like a lady, attend church, don't curse.

But my family's rules and societies expectations go hand in hand, and it's impolite to hold both.

Picture this.

We're strangers. Walking through each other like ghosts. Never passing one another, just through.

My eyes finding comfort in yours, your hands reaching out for me, almost touching my waist whenever we step into each other's bodies, but never quite.

Maybe you're too close, not enough space to hold me the way you want to... maybe you're just too nervous...

I know I always am when you enter me like a house with an unlocked door.

No knock, no warning.

Just an open, yet anticipated, visit.

Picture this.

We're friends. Sitting on an old swing set in your backyard.

There's ashes from where your shed burned down a week ago. You said it was old anyway. That you don't really care.

But we're friends, and I see the way you play with

your fingers when I ask if you're alright.

I see your eyes change, even though the sun set hours ago.

I see through you like a two-way mirror. I'm always looking in, sifting through blood and guts to find the pictures in your head. To make sense of whatever words are getting stuck in between your rib cage.

But you never see me.

You don't want to know what's behind your reflection. Or maybe you do. You've always had a hard time opening up to me.

Now picture this.

We're lovers. I fell for the veins that run like train tracks up your arms.

You said you've always admired my crooked tooth.

We talk in poetry. Dance like we're in a music video.

And we kiss too much, too sloppily, always leaving enough space in between to laugh, to smile, to fill the emptiness up with insignificant moments that will soon become our memories.

But memories fade, and people change, and life never waits. We kiss often, but it only lasts for a moment.

Picture this.

We're tired. Tired of the sun peeking in through the burgundy curtains that I picked out when we first moved in together.

You said you loved them, ran your palms along the fabric until I begged you to come to bed.

You used to run your hands along my spine, too. Lightly like a feather, yet heavy enough to make me feel wanted.

But I woke up with burn marks on my back the next morning and you just shrugged your shoulders. Said "I don't know" while rocking back and forth on your heels.

You sounded like a child that had just gotten caught. Doing what? I'm not sure. But that should have been my first warning. Maybe I'd always known it was. Maybe I was too naive to believe it, too stubborn to admit it to myself.

The curtains were on fire when I came back from the bathroom, but you didn't know where to point your finger this time. Instead you kept your hands to your side, letting the flames create a barrier between what was and what was left.

We were tired. And paranoid. Subtle, yet distinct. In love, but falling out. Together, but only because we didn't know how not to be.

Picture this.

We're strangers. Stepping out of the way to let the other board the train first. Never wanting to seem like we needed each other, because we didn't, it was always a want. An excuse to be held captive by something other than ourselves.

We're strangers with a past. A dusty history book left torn and untouched for years and years and years...

We're strangers again. Ghostly hands roaming the air for a hand to hold, a waist to caress. But there's nothing there, there never was.

Nothing close enough to grasp. Nothing left to hold on to.

Yes, picture this.

We're ex-lovers. Standing in a four-story building.
An apartment with one bed. Packing up what once
belonged.

Empty walls where your paintings once floated.
Empty shelves where my books once found safety
in between wooden frames.

And I find myself asking: "Is this what you want?
Are you just going to give up like that?"

My voice broke. The universe shattered. And you
looked through me. This time it killed me. This time
it was real.

You never opened your mouth, yet I waited for a
response that I was sure would never come.

But somewhere in your silence, while the ceiling
was crumbling all around us and the walls were
shaking and my heart was bleeding out in my hands,
I knew I had found my answer.

He held onto me just a bit too long when we hugged goodbye. As if he'd never see me again. As if I'd forget his name by tomorrow.

I knew I wouldn't answer his texts or anticipate a voicemail, but he didn't know that, and somehow that made all of this a little more painful.

I don't know how to casually visit friends, or look people in the eyes, or talk about the parts of me that escape when I'm stuck at a red light.

I don't know how to know when my feelings are strong, or strange, or both. I feel things in colors.

A subtle sky blue when it's three pm and I'm curled up on the couch watching Maury with my mom after she gets home from work.

A bright red when I see my old friends getting by without me. It's like I'm a ghost, or a shadow, or both. I'm just not alive in their eyes anymore.

We live in different universes even though the distance from me to them is only a block or two away.

A pale yellow when I'm sitting in class thinking about my future, and how dull the hallways are and how bright it is outside when the final bell rings.

A fluorescent orange when I'm blasting music over the speakers in my mom's car, speeding on a highway with all the windows down singing along until my heart doesn't know the difference between screaming and crying.

I don't know how to feel like other people feel. I can't just fall in love and call it quits when I disagree with their beliefs. Or the way they snort when they laugh. Or the way their cute little quirks are now just irritating patterns that get in the way of everything.

I can't just leave, so I never come in. If I never start, I'll never have to finish. It hurts less that way, I think. For the both of us.

And he held onto me just a bit too tightly when we hugged goodbye, but I let him.

He wanted to kiss me, but I lingered until my friend cleared her throat and reminded me that it was past curfew.

His hands around my waist made me never want to see him again, because they were rough, sturdy, safe. I liked dangerous and free. So I didn't answer his texts and I never waited up for a phone call. I just slept.

I don't remember his name anymore, and I hope that he never has to see me again, because that would feel a lot like a violent black, unpredictable and unsteady. And we'd both feel it, too.

We'd dress ourselves head to toe in that color until there was nothing left but the darkness to swallow us up.

I left home. Couldn't take it anymore. The yelling, the slamming of doors... it was too much.

She blamed it on her pregnancy, said she couldn't help it. I told her that I got it, that I understood, but all I wanted to say was "That doesn't mean you get to treat me like shit. It's not an excuse to blow up on me when I'm just trying to help you."

But I didn't, I didn't say that, because it wouldn't be fair to her... that's what I told myself to keep from throwing up every comment that I've managed to swallow down for so long.

And I got sick of it, so I left.

It wasn't safe to stay in a house while a candle burned in the corner of the room, curtains blowing around close enough to catch flame but never quite...

I said I wanted to be alone, didn't wait up for a response, and walked out of the house that smelled like tension instead of love...

I left the door unlocked on my way out.

I called my friend crying.

The restaurant across the street from me was closing and a man came out the side door. He saw my tears in the moonlight but was more focused on finding his car; I respected him for that. You can't save everyone but I couldn't fucking breathe.

My phone was pressed against my chest instead of my ear because I was embarrassed, embarrassed to be breaking down on the phone with someone that claimed to care but never showed it... and he thought that I was crying over him.

But I wasn't.

He was a scratch, everything else I was thinking about was a scar.

I tried to talk but I couldn't. He tried to listen but failed to hear me over the water running on his end of the line. He was brushing his teeth, getting ready to go to a party out of town. He told me to call him later...

I hung up, knowing that I wouldn't.

I stopped at a convenience store for coffee but ended up crying in the bathroom.

I was glad my face was bare. It's hard to hide mascara stains when they're painted down your cheeks.

I paid for the coffee and left, never even taking a sip before throwing the cup at a brick wall. I was proud of myself for not punching it instead. I'd rather waste my money than explain to people why my knuckles are bruised... they're all just curious anyways.

No one really sticks around long enough to hear the ending. Why would they?

I sat alone at an old train station.

Watched the cars drive by, took notice of the starless sky. I tried to exhale but my bottom lip was trembling. I bit it to stop myself from crying again.

Breathe out the anger... breathe out...

I tried to stay calm but the word felt so foreign. No one around me noticed that while their lives were moving forward, mine was frozen. Maybe they didn't get it... maybe I was in a different universe than them, maybe...

but I couldn't be the only one that felt like a storm tonight... someone out there was striking people with lightning instead of smiles, too.

The thought both saddened and relaxed me. I started walking again, letting the wind guide me.

A car slowed down next to me. Let them take me, I thought. But they didn't, they didn't.

My back was pressed against the wall of a funeral home.

I let my hand linger over the flame of a lighter just to feel something. But I felt nothing. Only heat... I wanted to burn.

I'm not living. I said this out loud, knowing that no one would hear me.

Everyone was either drunk or asleep... no one is happy, no one cares.

There was a furnace burning behind me... I could feel it through the cement walls and I thought, let it take me, come on... but it didn't. It didn't.

I went home.

Ran out of places to stain with my presence. Ran out of friends to call. Most didn't pick up, others said that I would be fine. Wasted breath, wasted time.

I didn't want to go home.

Didn't want to put the band aid back on a wound that was already healed. I wanted to be happy, content that I had a place to go when everything around me blew up in my face... but I wasn't happy. Everyone knew that.

And I left home because I couldn't take it anymore, but she needs me. I swear to god she needs me... and I'm starting to realize that the house I grew up in was never home but rather hell in disguise.

And I find myself sitting alone on the floor in my room most nights, back against the bedpost, wondering if I was in denial or if I was just too blind to notice the set of ashes under my pillow case every morning.

My mother is pregnant.

I am 18 years old.

My baby sister will grow up with a better understanding of technology than I have now.

It will be programmed in her mind before the age of seven and stay with her until the fragile age of seventy.

She will never understand the joys of a summer swim without the urge to check her phone every ten minutes, nor will she even acknowledge that she's doing it.

On top of this, she will struggle greatly before her sixteenth birthday, but that is a common occurrence amongst every teenager, it is normal.

It would be unheard of if she had a perfect life within the walls of an imperfect society.

I will be thirty-six by the time she is my age: the confusing age of eighteen.

The year of driving tests, boyfriends and college applications.

The year of heightened rebellion and loss of

innocence.

She will be the age I am now, but with more wit, more intelligence, and hopefully more confidence.

As her older sister, I will do everything in my power to prevent her from making the same mistakes that I have.

So I will tell her this: life is simple, it's the little details that are woven into your daily routines that make it complex.

"Being a teenager...," adults say with a nostalgic look on their faces, "...the best years of your life."

And they are usually right, but only if you find beauty in decay, laughter in sadness, warmth on chilly days, and love within the cracks of broken people.

It all has to do with your mindset and how you deal with situations that aren't always bright.

I will tell her that the hardest part about growing up is learning how to cope with unwanted visitors.

Monsters that don't shrink even when the lights

come on.

An illness can consume you, but only if you let it.

And so I will remind her to keep fighting and to stay strong.

To hold on even when times get so hard that she not only forgets how to breathe, but finds herself far too tired to even try.

I will tell her that being a teenager is growing up with the idea that you lack something someone else radiates.

Sometimes it takes medication, therapy, or even a couple of breakdowns to understand that, despite the urge to compare, life is not a competition.

Another girl's beauty is not the absence of your own... another student's A does not mean that you are stupid for getting a C.

These are just stepping stones that you're going to have to learn how to cross.

Instead of being envious of what someone else has, you should admire them for it.

Admire their hard work and dedication and use that

admiration to better yourself, to motivate yourself into becoming something greater, someone stronger.

I will tell my sister that self-love is a beautiful thing, and that the sooner you realize it, the easier life will be.

You're going to have to get used to hearing people say "Oh, they're just a teenager."

As if your age is all that you are.

As if your age dictates whether or not you're worthy of the advantages that come with being an adult.

As if "being a teenager" is a bad thing.

It's like you're almost there, but not quite.

Your teenage years are going to be rough, but I promise you that there will always be an abundance of positives as well.

This includes spontaneous decisions, more freedom, the ability to create unforgettable memories, and the opportunity to grow mentally and physically.

Growth is a beautiful thing; you should always accept it and feel confident enough to inspire others with it.

I will be sure to tell my baby sister that life is not short, not even close.

Living is a simple task, it's your actions that make it complicated.

So smile, laugh, photograph what intrigues you, eat when you're hungry, express your emotions, speak your mind, and always remember that you are something not everyone will know how to love, and that's okay.

"I don't really want to talk to you right now but sometimes what we want doesnt really matter, now does it?"

"you clearly just love bottling up all of your feelings till somebody finds out or they disappear."

"Tell me why youre mad."

"I mean you really cant get upset or anything"

"Atleast care if shes happy"

"oh and you said ""i know im drunk but this is the truth and it's something i would never say to you sober"""

"it came from the person who i honest to god, never even thought would say that no matter what happened."

"You called"

"You specifically told me to leave you alone and to fuck off so im respecting your wishes."

"You make no fucking sense alexa."

"Talk to me when youre done like cursing me out"

"Were both not stubborn people we just jumped the

gun to quick and you know this you even said it alexa remember?"

"You go to the party and i will not come and or talk to you"

"Give me some time to think how to word this alexa."

"Sorry, I can't talk right now. Call back later"

"ANSWER THE QUESTION ALEXA YES OR NO"

"Whenever youre drunk dont call me again i was so worried about you all night."

"she's better than you..."

"See you around"

- a compilation of the texts you both sent to me that night

I woke up one morning to the sound of my mother screaming so loud that the windows shook.

It scarred her throat, I think.

I know that she never really yelled unless something got to her, and I knew that it wasn't my fault this time because I was in my room, but I remembered that he was in hers.

The kitchen sink was filled with dishes that weren't even dirty.

No remnants of last night's dinner, not even a stain.

There was a bright yellow bowl sitting on the counter, our baking bowl, we liked to call it, because that was the bowl we used to mix the batter.

It wasn't empty, although I wished it was.

The pancakes were in a state of preparation, but that's all they'd ever be at this point.

Besides, I had lost my appetite, I'm sure my mother did, too.

The wooden spoon remained propped up against the left side of the bowl and my heart sank when I looked at it.

How do you go from making breakfast to breaking down into sobs?

Sunlight was coming in through the kitchen window but dark clouds threatened the hallway.

I swear I heard thunder rattle in the distance, but it was just the sound of his truck backing out of our driveway.

Two months later my mother and I are cleaning the house.

The radio's playing softly in the background and she's singing along until her phone interrupts the calmness that we've created.

I don't have to see the screen to know the name that's on it.

I don't have to trust that he'll be a better man this time.

He's said it before but there's still shards of glass on

the dining room carpet.

He's learned how to avoid it.

I think my mother just learned how to accept it.

I know what songs to skip when we're in the car running errands.

Her hands grip the steering wheel until her knuckles turn white and her eyes became distant, unfocused.

Almost like the lens on the camera she bought me for my fifteenth birthday.

Sometimes I look at the photographs I took of her smiling when I hear her crying in her room.

I can never bring myself to delete them because she is so beautiful, and I'm afraid that one day a man will make her forget it.

I know not to mention my father around her anymore because he told her to fuck off and to leave him alone.

I still blame myself for everything even though I'm told that I did nothing wrong.

My mother reminds me every day, she says "Baby, none of this is your fault" and "Your father's just an asshole."

"He doesn't deserve you."

I guess I just feel responsible for being the thing that holds them together, even though they fell apart years ago.

I know not to speak when she's breaking down in her bed at two in the morning because my grandmother doesn't support her pregnancy.

I know that I just need to hold her until her body stops shaking and she runs out of tears.

I know when it's okay to let go and when to excuse myself so I can bring her back the tissue box.

The breakdowns are so familiar now that I've memorized the routine.

It is one that I'll never miss a step on.

And I remembered back to that sunny morning a year and a half ago, and when I went into the kitchen this time the sink was empty, the dishes were stacked, and the yellow bowl was put away.

Sunlight came in through every window of the house and there were no dark clouds in the hallway, only a slight breeze that echoed when I walked by.

My mother doesn't cry like she used to and I don't wake up in the middle of the night anymore.

I think she's doing better.

I think she realized that the weight of a man does not make her weightless and that as long as her and I have each other, we have everything.

you kiss the concrete thinking that maybe gravel on
your tongue will hurt less than the goodbye that she
whispered into your mouth

you forge your signature on overdue hearts in hopes
that maybe they'll give you a good fucking instead
of a big "fuck off"

you play the victim in your own movie and always
forget to tell everyone who the villain is

you blame the girl that convinced you to drink for
fun because now it is a habit and you don't seem to
mind

you stutter over three wine glasses and smoke
enough cigarettes to fucking choke on your own
words

you don't remember that love is patient because all
you care about is pleasure and you'll do anything to
get what you want

you dodge the visions of her that surround your
hazy head at night and whisper to yourself

"i don't need you"

"i don't need you"

"i don't need you"

you wake up sober only to become high again

you wake up lonely only to force a stranger into
your bed

you wake up with thoughts of her and you can't
stand the fact that her tongue is down somebody
else's throat

and you finally call her

but all you get is the ongoing dial tone

Do you see that?

They're talking about you.

They're talking about the way you stuttered over your words in second period while doing a presentation.

You thought that you did pretty well, but you were wrong.

Do you hear that?

They're laughing at you.

They don't care who hears, they especially want you to hear.

They want you to feel embarrassed over the way you tripped while walking down the hallway.

You thought that no one noticed, but they did.

Do you feel that?

The shame, the guilt, the words "why me?" repeating over and over again in your head.

Do you feel that?

The heat rushing to your face, the nervousness in your stomach, the tap tap tapping of your fingers against your thigh as you try to appear casual, like nothing is wrong.

Like everything is okay.

Everything is okay.

Are you okay?

Yeah, I'm okay.

Do you feel that?

The strong sense of hopelessness, the never-ending sting of failure?

Do you know that no one's really talking about you?

That the group of girls walking by are more focused on their nail polish chipping than the outfit you chose to wear today.

Do you know that everyone gets afraid to speak in front of the class sometimes?

That by the time you finish and sit back down everyone has already forgotten what you were talking about.

Do you know those voices that you hear?

The one's that don't make sense, the one's that speak loudly but slowly, the incoherency practically dripping off of every syllable.

Do you know what I'm talking about?

Are you familiar with the darkness?

Have you become friends with the stars?

Are you okay?

I always am.

Are you sure?

Yes.

Are you tired of the voices?

Do they get too loud at night?

Do you know how to turn them off?

You can't.

They don't like the feeling of loneliness, they don't like to speak if no one's listening.

And I've never been good with friendships or the act of communication, so tell me, who am I supposed to confide in when the voices in my head won't even be my friend?

ask me to stay

when the storm outside threatens to drown you

when the thunder itself is enough to sound you

ask me to stay

when you're in times of fear

when the feeling of loneliness gets too severe

ask me to stay

when you're surrounded by pain

when you're struggling to exhale the intake of rain

ask me to stay

when the bottle kisses your lips

when you remember those moments

you swore you'd never miss

ask me to stay

when her hands are on your chest

when you're playing with her hair

to ease your mind's mess

ask me to stay

when you feel better off alone

when you scream my name through an empty house

and realize that i'm not home

time cannot heal what wounds i have made

for i've left so many scars

and they won't seem to fade

and i know that apologies are often short

but i'm willing to add length

if it'll somehow mean more

and i'm sorry for the damage that i've left behind

for i swear i'm not messy

just afraid of the crime

and i know that running will not take me away

but what am i to do when i don't know what to say

and the aftermath is growing

but i don't know where to turn

for a collision of wrong doings surely does burn

and i know that a fire cannot start without a spark

so i guess i'm to blame for the flames in my heart

hazy hazy hazy i've forgotten how to breathe

the destruction of our delicacy is tugging on my
sleeve

and i feel as though i'm clawing at a surface that
won't budge

i'm gasping for the distant air but all i get is mounds
of blood

and i keep trying to rid my mind of all the tattered
thoughts of you

but every time you say hello it's like an attempt at
something new

and i promise that i'm doing okay

but i can't help to dream of us

and maybe it's not you that i miss but rather the
craving of someone's love

and i can't help but start a downpour when i
remember back to the months

it's like you never really were there so why does
your absence hurt so much

and i can swear to you that i'm happy

and that i'll smile when you've moved on

but the simple thought of her touching you will
haunt me even after i'm gone

i'm sitting alone because i don't know how not to be alone

my friends laugh but i just break

they talk in rhythm but i'm always off key

they look radiant, blooming

next to them i am nothing but a deteriorating flower disguised by a human body

i rot, and everyone flees because why stand next to someone that's decaying when you could bathe yourself in the light of happiness

i can't feel anything

people keep walking by but no one looks long enough to see the hollowness behind my eyes or the way my hands are shaking from lack of sleep, lack of food, lack of life

i'm drowning here on this stupid bench and people just keep wading through the waves

i'm sitting alone because that's how it's always been

i can't hold a conversation and eye contact makes

me nervous and no one wants to waste their time
staying still when they could be out thriving

i'm tired

people keep telling me that this is college

that this is college

that it's supposed to be hard

that things will get easier

that every negative thought i have will stick to this
fucking bench and wither away in time because i
don't need to carry around that kind of pessimism

but i do

i do

and it hurts

can you tell me when it won't

you're going to cry and people aren't going to care.

you'll be sitting on a bench by yourself at 1:13 am with a book next to you because you thought that you could keep yourself together long enough to focus on someone else's words instead of on your thoughts but you can't because your head is loud and the world is quiet and no one is going to walk by and ask if you're okay.

you'll be at a diner at 4:06 am in a booth meant for two but instead of someone sitting across from you there will only be another menu a reminder a storm not yet in motion an echo of your loneliness that is taking form in the shape of mockery and lack of reassurance to destruct any progress you've made on convincing yourself that you're not alone and that things are okay... but they aren't okay and you really are alone.

you're going to cry you're going to cry and people aren't going to notice and they aren't going to care.

you're going to cry you're going to fall apart and you are going to break your own fucking heart.

but just be tough... be tough. be strong enough to touch the damage without retreating, strong enough to let yourself in without fleeing... cry, okay? but don't let yourself drown.

He'll talk about getting a hotel room with you.

Say shit like "I can see the pain in your eyes."

Let you read him your poetry.

Pretend that he's listening to your heartbeat when really he's just trying to get underneath your shirt.

He'll talk about drinking wine with you.

Conversations instead of sleep.

Say "just the two of us" until you can't stop thinking about it.

He'll take you to the edge of New York.

Close enough to see but too far to touch.

Kind of like him.

He's there, telling you that you look beautiful despite the humidity, despite feeling ugly in the presence of such a radiant city, but he's distant.

Always out of reach.

He'll hold your hand while he drives.

Blast the air cause he's sweating but turn it down

when he sees the goosebumps on your arms.

Open the windows instead.

Offer to let you drive his truck but never give you the keys.

He'll talk about trips to the mall and let you buy him his favorite coffee because he likes knowing that you remembered what it is.

Talk about the future even though he doesn't want one with you yet.

He'll start to ignore your calls.

Watch your drunk texts flood his phone screen before turning it over and draining it.

He'll say "I've got a lot going on."

Make you wait up for him even though he's already asleep.

Get sick on the thought that he's not talking to you because he's fucking someone else.

Cause you to wonder what the fuck happened.

Why everything changed so fast.

He'll say that he misses walking around with you at night.

Tell you that he wants to kiss you and call you his before hanging up and disappearing for another two days.

You'll tell him that it's okay, that you'll wait for him because he's different... but you shouldn't.

His absence will lead to tears that he won't acknowledge, won't even see.

You'll feel heartbroken and wonder why you let yourself fall that fast for a boy who doesn't even know your favorite color.

He'll talk about getting an apartment with you.

What it would be like to share a cigarette in the city.

How bad he wants to touch you.

Take you out on dates.

Kiss you in the rain and then leave you there.

Make you fall for him again and again and again and then act like you're the one who ruined everything.

He'll play the victim...

don't let him think that he is.

it was real

it happened

i was there

and it feels like a dream, you and me

you touched me in the back seat because i let you,
needed you to distract me from the thoughts that i
could never fucking kill

we found the darkest dead end this town had to
offer and drove around for an hour before putting
the truck in park

i touched you in the backseat because you let me,
needed me to take your mind off of the fact that
your ex was fucking someone else

i didn't love you; i barely even knew you, but
somehow i fell for you

let your words convince me that you weren't like
everyone else, that you weren't going to hurt me
after i told you how many times people have broken
me and left me to bleed out, that you were just as
scared as i was to start over with someone new

and you knew that you were going to leave me, too;
kept it stored in the back of your mind so i'd never
find it whenever i tried to figure you out

you stopped answering me, stopped caring

i still don't understand why

and i was pathetic for trying to patch up the distance
between us when all i kept doing was falling in

i should have stopped there, should have accepted
the bruises instead of thinking that i was strong
enough to endure more

and i was there

it happened

it was real, you know

i still think about why you lied to me sometimes,
and how your shitty explanations left me with more
questions than i had before you even picked up the
damn phone

your jacket is still on top of my dresser

i was hoping that you'd come back for it because now my whole room smells like you and i don't know whether to cry or grieve over someone that's still alive

the last thing you said to me was

"i'll come another night okay"

but it's been three weeks, and you're not coming, and i'm not really surprised by that anymore, but for some reason i keep waiting around for you, keep writing about you

i guess i'm just trying to keep your ghost alive

Honestly?

People will ignore you.

Let you see the broken parts of who they are so that you feel responsible for fixing them - and then they will leave.

No warning, no explanation.

Just a lot of heartache and headaches.

Learn to put yourself first.

Honestly?

You'll fuck up.

Maybe drink too much and kiss too many boys and girls.

Maybe say something you don't mean.

Maybe lose a friend in the process of finding yourself.

It's okay, just keep learning.

Never stop growing.

Honestly?

Sometimes midnight lasts for days.

It's dark and you're alone and you can't stop
thinking about how much everything has changed.

Get up, turn on the light.

Have enough strength to kill the monsters under
your bed.

Honestly?

You'll wake up next to a stranger someday.

Someone you used in order to forget about the
someone who broke you.

It won't feel good, you might regret it, you'll leave
and forget to lock the door behind you, you'll still
think about the one who made you feel like you had
to do this in order to move on.

Don't use sex to hide the fact that you're just really
fucking lonely, face it.

Deal with it.

Honestly?

Just be honest.

Say what you feel, do what you think is right.

Not everyone is going to like you, what matters most is that you like you.

Fuck the rest, just be real.

Love every word that comes out of your mouth... because it means nothing if you don't.

Highways.

Never taking backroads.

Why would we? It's so lonely on them. We've taught ourselves to avoid those kinda paths.

The Maine blasting through speakers that don't belong to the driver... but he makes them his own.

Makes us passengers feel safe even when he hits 80.

Hand on my thigh.

Seat belt tucked behind my back so I can put my head out the window, taste the wind, knot my hair on purpose, let the smoke from my cigarette cloud my sad thoughts, let it blur them out completely.

Teenagers that should be doing homework. Teenagers that should be sleeping, not eating out at expensive diners with money we haven't earned. Money we can't afford to spend.

Hand on my thigh.

He watches me instead of the road.

Thinks I don't notice, but I always do.

Instead of feeling anxious I feel alive.

Instead of feeling reckless I feel revived.

Strangers that became passengers that became kids again.

My friends screaming song lyrics in the backseat until they lose their voice.

Our own personal concert, I like to think.

His hand on my head, fingers getting lost in the knots of my hair.

One handed driving.

He's so good at that.

Late night bowling alleys that look cheap but make us feel rich.

Rich on adventure.

The night never ends, even when it does.

It's like a song on repeat, the melody never changes but the days do.

We just find new music to play when we get tired of living through old memories.

He kisses me and tells me that I taste like the desert he just watched me eat.

Stares at me when I put on my makeup and tells me that I'm beautiful rather than telling me that I don't need it.

Makes me feel comfortable both naked or clothed, both drunk or sober.

Highways on Monday nights when we should be studying.

Freedom.

Lack of hurt.

More love.

All love.

His hand in mine, my friends by my side.

Laughter.

Smiles.

Smoke.

Dark red nails instead of black.

Love.

He smiles and says "you think too much about yourself..."

So how do I convince him that he's the only thing on my mind these days?

the minute i become comfortable with happiness is the second i lose it. it's a cycle, you know? but i always choose it. i know the consequences, i know that whatever happens will probably end up hurting me, but i go for it anyway, cause sometimes i just wanna see if things will be different, if somehow everything will change, but life likes to laugh in my face most of the time, and i never know what to say. i never know what to say.

I touched him first, and I'm sorry if that hurts you, but it's not his fault that we started making promises without intention to keep them, it's not his fault that we fell apart... it's not mine, either.

Treat him kindly, leave lipstick stains on his cheek and kisses down his chest. You'll find ashes under his covers some nights because I know that he still burns for me, sometimes I still burn for him, too, but I've learned how to put the fire out before destroying everything around me... he just lets it die down on its own and covers the burns with band aids.

I'm sorry that I had to end it, I'm sorry that I had to put us out, but every time I breathed you in it tasted like smoke instead of fresh air.

I loved him first even though I knew I wouldn't love him last, and that's okay, because when she's moaning his name into his ear at midnight he'll whisper mine.

He'll whisper mine.

And I'll leave my window open so I can hear the way that he longs for me, even though I know that I will never lay next to him again.

But I don't want to think about that anymore, I don't want to let myself be hurt by the idea of him anymore.

So I won't. I won't. And this is where I begin my healing.

(do you ever miss the place you swore you hated?)

my heart is back home

here? it is dusty, tired, used

it lies in my mother's arms

she feels its shallow beats whenever she holds my sister

but our hearts cannot intertwine, my sister and i

because she is small, fragile, innocent

and i am broken, lost

i have seen too much, i have heard too much, i have felt too much

i would never expose my sister to a thunderstorm without her knowledge of rain

i would never break her down before she even learns how to build herself back up

she creates her own luck, and i am unlucky

i would shatter if our worlds ever touched

my heart lies beneath my mother's smile

in between the bags under her eyes and the pieces of gray hair becoming more and more present with age

but she is so beautiful, and she keeps my heart beautiful, and i could never ask for a love greater

my heart can be found in pieces

for it is not whole, it never has been

i don't know why

there are parts of me that take refuge in my old little town

find a corner sitting peacefully on the train tracks, smoking a cigarette, talking to friends that never quite understood but still listened

find a middle piece in the parking lot of wawa

spending her mother's money on peanut m&ms and sweet tea, even though she knows that she shouldn't be burning holes through paper that she hasn't earned, paper that she can't afford to spare

find jagged edges sleeping in the backseat of
different guys' cars, feeling a little lonely even in
the presence of strong arms and raspy voices,
realizing that she is crying on the ride home the next
morning because this is not right, this is not who
she is

she shouldn't be lying next to boys who don't even
ask about her dreams upon waking up

she shouldn't be begging for attention, affection,
love, when she knows that it will end up burning
her in the end

my scars haven't healed yet, but neither have the
memories

my heart is back home

here? it is in hiding, but no one has bothered to
search for it

why? i don't know

does it make me sad? no

find a part so small that you may miss it the first
time resting softly on an old couch in her father's

living room

he says to it "watch your siblings for a minute"

but disappears for hours

he says to it "why do you stay up so late"

knowing that he is the reason for her nightmares

he says to it "if i ever catch you smoking i will kill you"

(do it, god dammit)

find the remains of this already shrinking heart two years later, standing in front of her father's apartment, lighting up a cigarette with her middle finger up in an attempt to communicate with a man that remains hidden behind brick walls and locked doors

unresponsive man inside... he never comes out

he does not want to see the mess of a young woman
he does not want to see his broken daughter
he does not want to be held responsible for causing that kind of damage

so he plays the victim, because it's what he's best at

my heart is scarred, torn

put your hand on my chest and you will feel
nothing; that's what i've been told

no heartbeat, no pulse

just a pair of dark eyes and a bloody soul

find pieces of my heart scattered on the grounds that
i have walked on

find it clinging to the palms of old friends, past
lovers, strangers that i have had conversations with
on the train but never addressed by their names

find it burning, let it burn, watch it burn

don't you dare try to put out a fire that isn't ready to
settle down yet, don't you dare try and threaten me

my heart is back home

here? it is dusty, tired, used, abandoned, mistreated,
ignored

here, i don't exist. here, i don't wish to

AUTHOR'S NOTE

"a ghost's pageant"

"You, being the ghost, a pageant being, there are typically different people. And throughout these poems, you were feeling a different sort of way every time. So within each of these poems it's you walking down the runway each time."

Thank you, Bobby, for not only creating the title for my book, but for always being my poetry pal. May your words be heard by many.

You have just read five years worth of poetry.

Five years worth of a lot of heartbreak and a little love. A lot of tears and so little happiness.

But I am healing. I am no longer burning.

Please, let my words resonate with you. Let them be a shoulder to lean on when you feel tired and alone.

Please, be strong, and grow with me.

71857732R00183